The RCAF
As Seen From the Ground

Alexander Velleman

The RCAF
As Seen From the Ground
(A Worm's-Eye View)

Book One: The War Years
1939 - 1945

Alexander Velleman, EM, CD
Warrant Officer, RCAF (Retired)

CANADA'S WINGS, INC.

The RCAF as Seen From the Ground

Copyright © 1986 Alexander Velleman

No part of this book may be reproduced or transmitted in any form by any means, electric or mechanical, in print or electronic media, including photocopying and recording, or by an information storage or retrieval system, without the written consent of the author, except for brief passages quoted by a reviewer.

Published in Canada by
Canada's Wings, Inc.
Box 700, Stittsville
Ontario, K0A 3G0

in co-operation with
Alexander Velleman

Printed in Canada by Les Editions Marquis Ltee., Montmagny, Quebec. Book design by Heather Ebbs, Nepean, Ontario. Cover drawing and line drawings in book by Johanna James, Brampton, Ontario. Cartoons by Stephen Neese, Oakville, Ontario. Photos and newspaper clippings are in the author's possession.

Canadian Cataloguing in Publication Data

Velleman, Alexander, 1919-
The RCAF as seen from the ground

Contents: bk. 1. The war years, 1939-1945.
ISBN 0-920002-32-3 (v. 1)

1. Velleman, Alexander, 1919- 2. Canada.
Royal Canadian Air Force--Biography.
I. Title.

UG635.C3V44 1986   358.4'0092'4   C86-090077-0

*This book is dedicated
to my son, Robbie,
who made it necessary for me to write it,
and to my wife, Es,
who was patient throughout the time it took to write.*

Contents

	Foreword	1
1	**Manning Depot, Toronto** December 1939 - January 1940......................	.3
2	**RCAF Station, Rockcliffe** February 1940 - February 1941	.9
3	**No. 3 Bombing & Gunnery School, Macdonald, Manitoba** March 1941 - October 1944	.33
4	**No. 3 Wireless School, Winnipeg** October 1944 - December 1944	.78
5	**No. 15 Service Flying Training School, Claresholm, Alberta** January 1945 - February 1945	.84
6	**No. 5 Radio School, Clinton, Ontario** March 1945 - June 1945	.93
7	**No. 10 Service Flying Training School, Souris, Manitoba** July 1945 - August 1945.........................	.106
	Epilogue	111
	Glossary	113

Foreword

THESE BOOKS ARE NOT INTENDED as a military treatise, but rather as the memoirs, or memories, of a typical RCAF ground tradesman, as he travelled with the RCAF through and after the war. This is a view of the events that occurred at the various RCAF establishments where he was stationed, as he recollects them. No doubt there are tens of thousands of these stories: this one tells of a young man who entered the RCAF in 1939 as an Aircraftman 1st Class (AC1) and a Wireless Operator Electrical Mechanic (WOEM) Group C, and who retired in 1966 as a Warrant Officer, Telecommunications Maintenance Superintendent Ground, Group 4 (TelMSupt(G)4).

It should be appreciated that to a young man entering such a service, it appeared that the RCAF (pre-war) was little other than an Officers' Flying Club. True, they did a little mapping and search and rescue for the federal government, but the emphasis was on flying. Some of the officers who flew the aircraft didn't know, or appear to care, who serviced their aircraft, or how, as long as they were indeed serviced. Others got their act together quickly, and realized that without an efficient and effective ground staff, they were dead in the air. Ground staff, of course, did all the menial tasks; besides servicing the aircraft and their various necessities, they handled messing, quarters, paperwork, and so forth. To those airmen who cleaned up their act, I raise my civilian cap, or in military jargon, *those I salute!*

There are a good many incidents that have been forgotten, others have been intentionally left out. There are no apologies offered for either, but, needless to say, those incidents were not too relevant to the writing of this book, or they would have been included.

These books are divided into the various stations, establishments, schools, and other units to which I was transferred, posted, seconded, or attached, or placed on temporary duty with. Names have been changed to enable the bearers to remain anonymous.

Book One recalls the war years, beginning in September 1939 and ending in mid-1945, V-J Day.

Alexander Velleman
Oakville, 1985

1
Manning Depot, Toronto
December 1939 - January 1940

MY FIRST RECOLLECTION OF THE RCAF is rather vague. I can remember standing in front of a desk, at which sat a very young pilot officer, at the RCAF Recruiting Office. I was still in army uniform, sporting the sergeants' stripes that I had worked so hard all summer to confirm. I had been at Camp Petawawa in the summer of 1939, had qualified as a gun sergeant with the Royal Canadian Artillery, and had received two weeks' leave: the last week of August and the first week of September. I was then to report to the 2nd Montreal Regiment as a signals instructor. However, in the first week of September, before my leave expired, I received a wire instructing me to report to the regiment immediately, as war had been declared and the unit was to be mobilized. I was to be attached to the 27th Field Battery as their Signals Sergeant. They had the old 4.5 howitzers, and were to retrain on the newer 25-pound field guns instead.

Reporting there, I was advised by the RSM (Regimental Sergeant Major) that my new Commanding Officer was a Major Keil, and that the BSM (Battery Sergeant Major) was a WO2 Feal. I checked in, and was informed that the Place Viger Hotel, east of the armouries on the south side of Craig Street, was to be our barracks. They were not yet ready, but would be soon; until that time I was to live out on subsistence. My signals detachment of 12 men was not my only responsibility, as I was to teach the new three's drill as well.

The Place Viger Hotel was soon considered ready, but it was still a rather dreary place. At one time it had been a very grand establishment, but it had been neglected for many years, and the neglect showed. The engineers had been on the job, so the water ran, the heat (which we did not yet need) worked, and so on, but there was no furniture.

There were no commercial double-decker bunks yet available in Montreal, so the engineers manufactured some with two-by-fours and chicken wire. There were mattresses of course, and blankets, but no sheets or pillowslips, though we had pillows. The men slept ten to a room, and the senior NCOs (non-commissioned officers, a sergeant or higher in the enlisted ranks) slept two to room. The men used the corridor washrooms, and the senior NCOs had *en suites.*

My girlfriend Es and I had decided some time earlier to get married in November 1939, so I requested official permission and asked to be placed on the married establishment. This meant that I would receive the married allowance, and thus entitle Es to all the financial benefits of being a married serviceman's wife. Permission was granted, and we soon made the necessary arrangements with Reverend Stafford of St. James United Church on St. Catherine Street in Montreal. Es asked one of her girlfriends to be there as bridesmaid, and I arranged to have the BSM and one of the gun sergeants there as best man and witness. The arrangements worked out quite well, and we were married. We had a whole weekend to ourselves before Es returned to work on Monday and I returned to the regiment.

A point of explanation here: I was, at that time, an avid amateur radio buff, and I talked by Morse key and shortwave radio with other amateurs around the world. In "ham", or amateur radio language, "es" was used as an abbreviation for the word "and". My girlfriend's full name was Estrecia; there is no need, I believe, for further explanation for my abbreviating her name!

Es was about my age, and she held a passion for the piano. She was well on her way to becoming a concert pianist, and she worked at a library and taught piano to support the lessons she needed to achieve her goal. She was slight, and I would guess that she didn't weigh more than 100 pounds soaking wet. She was completely ignorant of the trials and tribulations that she was in for as a service wife and hadn't even been given the opportunity to learn how to cook. That was all to change, very soon!

Rumours abounded, and we had all sorts of stories about when we would be going overseas. We were to be part of the First Canadian Contingent. I had been taken off Regular Force rates of pay and placed on CASF (Canadian Active Service Force) rates. These lower rates were brought into effect by the Army soon after mobilization.

On December 6th, 1939, I was called into the CO's office and notified that the 27th Field Battery was changing weapons. It was to become an anti-tank unit, and as these did not use signals personnel, I would have the choice of staying with the battery and going on to guns, or transferring to another unit that could make use of my signals expertise. I had no liking for guns, and decided that transfer would be more suitable for me.

I expected to be transferred to another unit in the regiment, but not so: I was given a letter of introduction and sent off to the RCAF Recruiting Centre. And thus I came to be standing before that young pilot officer mentioned earlier.

I was to be sworn in as an AC1 (Aircraftman 1st Class), Group C, because of my military experience. Till then I had known only the Army, and had absolutely no knowledge of the boys in blue. They appeared to have very little tradition, and I knew nothing of their ranks, insignia, or even their protocol. Because of my escorting sergeant's attitude, and because he saluted when he entered the room, I guessed that the pilot officer was indeed an officer, but I could see no epaulettes nor rank badges of any kind. I did notice a thin, light-blue line above his sleeve cuff. He also wore wings above the left breast pocket. The ranks were perhaps my biggest problem. NCO ranks I could understand, except that they called their Staff Sergeants Flight Sergeants (or, in deference to the RAF, Chieffie). As in the Army, the warrant officers were addressed by mister, but the RCAF also called them major, whereas in the Army, major was an officer rank. The RCAF officer ranks left me cold. What was a pilot officer?—a pilot? Then there were flying officers; did these officers fly? There were flight lieutenants and so forth—all very confusing.

Then there were the uniforms. The sergeant who escorted me wore an open-necked tunic, with shirt and tie. So did the pilot officer, though there appeared to be a little difference in the material. Did all enlisted men wear a uniform similar to what the sergeant wore? The sergeant and I had lunch together at Murray's Restaurant in the University Towers Building (on the RCAF, with meal tickets), and I had the opportunity to find out a great deal.

After lunch I was issued with a transportation warrant, which I could turn in at the railway station for tickets and, to my amazement, meals and a berth! This was for my trip to Toronto, where I was to report to a place called Manning Depot at the Canadian National Exhibition Grounds. I was to receive my uniform and kit there and then wait for a transfer to a unit. I would also, no doubt, be given an indoctrination into the mysteries of the RCAF.

I hurried up to Outremont (a suburb of Montreal) to see my wife of little more than a month and to advise her of my change of status, and she appeared to be quite happy about it. That night I left for Toronto, and I enjoyed the trip and the possibility of a brand new career.

As I was reporting in the only clothing I had, my Army uniform, I was immediately asked if I knew the new three's drill. When the Discips (RCAF nomenclature for drill sergeants) found out that I not only knew it, but had just completed a course at Petawawa, I was told that I would be teaching three's drill until I was transferred out. I was to wear my Army uniform daytimes, and my RCAF uniform evenings and while off the base. That decided, I was then kitted out, and I was astounded by the array of goodies that were being issued. There were two complete, open-necked uniforms, four shirts with eight detachable collars, two pairs of boots, one pair of shoes, a pair of gloves, a greatcoat, two wedge caps, cap badges, button sticks, shaving kit with six blades (more about the six blades later), handkerchiefs, and underwear. There was even a tailor on hand in the event something didn't quite fit properly. This was quite unlike my experience with the Army. For bedding, a bunk was assigned me, with (of course) a mattress. A pair of blankets, a pair of sheets, a pillow, and a pillowslip were then issued! I had already been issued with two towels. I was to live in the lap of luxury! I could now understand why they called us The Gentlemen of The Royal Canadian Air Force.

The best deal was the pay. When I reported in early September to the Craig Street armouries, I was almost immediately placed on CASF rates of pay. This worked out to a basic $1.10 per diem, plus whatever trades pay one qualified for, and, naturally, increments for rank. I was then earning about $1.95 per day, plus subsistence (if applicable). As an AC1 C Group, on PAAF (Permanent Active Air Force) rates of pay, I was earning about $2.45. Thus, I was getting more pay and greater real benefits as an AC1 in the RCAF than I had received in the Army as a sergeant—at least, as far as creature comforts were concerned.

As there had been no Sergeants' Mess *per se* at the Place Viger Hotel, and only a small Regimental Mess at the Craig Street armouries, I really didn't miss the Mess when I arrived at Manning Depot in Toronto. Of course, there were some small disadvantages. I had to listen to the usual squawkers who complained about everything, though they probably never had it so good before in their lives. There were always some who found fault with everything and anything. As a senior NCO in the Army, I had been partly insulated against this sort of thing. Now it was brought to bear. Generally, however, Manning Depot was an experience I would not have missed for anything in the world. In my capacity as a drill sergeant daytimes and an AC1 in the evenings, I enjoyed a most peculiar position!

Most of December 1939 I spent as a drill instructor, and just before Christmas I was granted leave till New Year's Day. I travelled to Montreal in my RCAF uniform, sporting one of those PF winter fur caps (similar to those the Mounties wear). Those caps were withdrawn a year later, and I never saw them again during the rest of my RCAF career. On arrival in Montreal, I called my wife Es on the telephone and then called home to my folks, who lived in Dorval, to arrange for Es to spend my leave with me at their home. The short leave was over too soon, and Es and I parted in the Windsor railway station in Montreal in January 1940, not knowing when we might see each other again.

I had no sooner reported back to Manning Depot than I learned I had been attached to a squad detailed to guard the No. 400 (City of Toronto) Squadron Headquarters on Jarvis Street in Toronto. We were to guard the building for a week or so, as the squadron was being, or had been, shipped out. Why would we guard an old building that was undoubtedly vacated? Who were we to guard it against? The prostitutes who covered Jarvis Street like a blanket? Beds were shipped in, and we were assured that we would be catered the meals we needed. The meals indeed arrived, on time, and HOT. Clean linen arrived as well, and life really wasn't all that bad.

We then had the opportunity to look at what we were guarding, and a few things became evident. The squadron had left in a hurry, and even though there wasn't any equipment lying about, there was a great deal of paperwork. Army co-operation data was scattered all over the place. As an ex-Army man, who had worked at observation posts with the artillery, I could appreciate it perhaps a little better than the others. I had done quite a bit of gun laying in the past summer, and knew the importance of the job that an efficient Army co-operation squadron could do for artillery batteries.

There are many things that happen to us during a lifetime which we remember at the strangest times. Today, whenever I see a member of the Salvation Army, I think of the many dedicated souls who manned the Sally Ann canteen at the CNE grounds in Toronto in 1939 and 1940. To the thousands of sailors, soldiers, and airmen who spent some time at Manning Depot, these people were a real Godsend. Many men were not as lucky as I, and arrived there long before their documents. (I had brought mine with me from Montreal—one of the benefits, I guess, of having been a sergeant in the Army!) Until the necessary information arrived, these men could not receive full pay, only advances, and could not be kitted. Now, the Mess did provide excellent food, and in great quantities, but not coffee whenever you wanted it, nor doughnuts. The canteens did, but at a price, all except the Sally Ann. Coffee and doughnuts were always available at the Sally Ann, as were envelopes, paper, pens, and even stamps if you needed them. There was never any request for money, though a sign at the door said that if any patron could afford it, they would appreciate assistance in helping others. There was never any attempt to convert anyone, but there was always someone there to listen to your problems, and to assist you in any way he could—and he would! Whenever there is a fund drive today, I'm strongly biased toward the Sally Ann and away from the others, so many of which were Goody-Two-Shoes until the crunch came.

Orders came through soon, and a group of us with previous communications experience (mostly licensed radio amateurs) and classed as WOEMs were posted to Rockcliffe near Ottawa. Some were assigned to station signals, others to communication squadron (CommSqn), and I was one of the latter. When I had been issued my first RCAF transportation warrant at Montreal on enlistment, I had thought they were putting me on, giving me a berth as well as meals. Yet here I was, several months later—I was in, and there was no getting out—and I was again issued a transportation warrant which included meals and a berth—more proof that we were indeed The Gentlemen of the Royal Canadian Air Force!

It wasn't long before we were on our way to our first real Air Force station. Perhaps we would at last do more than guard an abandoned, or rather, vacated, building in the heart of Toronto's red light district! The train trip was uneventful, marked only by the continuous speculative chatter about our new station and what we might soon be doing. Only time would tell, and after a rather fitful night's sleep, we arrived at Ottawa's Central Station, to be met by RCAF transport and taken to Station Rockcliffe.

2
RCAF Station, Rockcliffe
February 1940 - February 1941

ON ARRIVAL AT ROCKCLIFFE, we were instructed by the Orderly Room that we were to live out. We would have to find accommodation and meals for ourselves, but to compensate, we would be given an allowance over and above our pay. Transportation would be provided from the end of the public transport line to the RCAF station. What we chose to pay for our accommodation was left entirely to us. We were, in effect, on our own. I had experienced this before, but some of the boys had some rather grandiose ideas and promptly went broke. The group of us assigned to CommSqn decided to stick together, and we chose a place from those listed on the accommodations board in the guard house. Our new home was far from grand, but it was well within our allotted budget, was near the centre of town, and was close to public transportation. We settled in, and I made arrangements for my wife to move in when she arrived.

The next morning we were picked up by the RCAF transport and, along with the balance of the personnel who lived out, were driven to Station Rockcliffe for our first day's work. When we reported to the Orderly Room, we were immediately commandeered (shanghaied might be a better word) by a little tin-god sergeant. Sgt Stese was a GD; we weren't familiar with this trade classification, but we quickly came up with a meaning for the letters. (The actual designation is General Duties, which involves everything from sweeping the floors or cleaning pots to issuing blankets for the Barrack Warden. Strangely enough, the General Duties list is a very respected branch in the officer bracket and normally in the aircrew branch as well!)

Sgt Stese herded us toward the main barracks, where he had his office (which was little more than a closet). Here he told us we would be working for him for some time and that we could either do as he told us or not, but if the latter, we would be very sorry indeed. He could be very tough with us, and the end result would be that we did the work for him anyway, so we might as well make up our minds to follow his instructions. We were quite disillusioned, to say the very least.

Again, I used some of the expertise I had gained in the Army and asked to be sent to the Sergeants' Mess as a waiter. Most of the boys thought I was nuts, but I stood my ground and eventually got the job. At the appropriate time I reported to the Sergeants' Mess. Having learned which table was used by the CommSqn senior NCOs, I wangled the job of waiting at that table. Lunchtime came, and I served my table well, using the opportunity to look for the wireless spider insignia that would indicate which of the NCOs was involved with the wireless trade. I was somewhat surprised to see that it was a white-haired, elderly looking sergeant who wore the spider insignia (which was finally dropped in 1945), but after looking more closely, I realized that he was actually about 25 years old with prematurely white hair.

At dinner that evening I managed to almost upset a bowl of the steaming hot soup in that poor sergeant's lap. He started into a tongue-lashing, as I had expected, and I was ready for him. Apologizing, I explained that I was no waiter, but a WOEM who had been shanghaied into the job by some GD sergeant in the barracks. I was careful to mention that I wasn't alone; there was a draft of us, all doing jobs other than those we were qualified and paid for. The wireless sergeant warned me to be more careful the next time and told me to carry on. But as he left the Mess later, he said I was to check at the guard house the next morning to see if my group's assignment had been changed.

I was elated at my success, and on the way home that night I told the rest of the group what had happened. When I mentioned the possibility of a change of orders the next morning, the boys all joshed about, sure that NOTHING worked that fast, not even in the Air Force. I held my peace, though I felt that somehow, things were working in our favour. I had an idea that a certain GD sergeant was getting an earful right about then from the CommSqn wireless sergeant or his superior.

The next morning, our second day at Rockcliffe, we caught the transport as before and were dropped off at the guard house. To the surprise of everyone but myself, there was indeed a change in orders, at least for those of us who were attached to CommSqn. Transport was waiting to take us to the CommSqn hangar, which was across the main field and runways some distance from the administrative area. Sgt Howe, my "victim" of the previous evening, greeted us when we arrived and gave us instructions concerning where and how we would get our issue tool kits from the supply people. Those tricks I had learned in the Army seemed to be universally useful, and I imagined they would see me through a few more tight predicaments. I wasn't about to forget what it had taken five years of Army training to learn.

Before we were allowed to work in the squadron, each of us was to have a full medical and dental examination. I knew I had no medical problems, and my Army paybook proved that I had any of the necessary shots and so on, but I was a little worried about the dental examination. The medical and dental personnel attached to the RCAF at that time were all members of the Army Medical or Dental Corps. (This was changed soon afterward for the medical types, but the Army Dental Corps continued to serve with the RCAF until at least 1966.) Both Corps honoured my Army paybook as if it were gold, but the Dental Corps did extract a bad tooth, leaving me with a gaping hole in the front of my smile. Oh well, it could have been much worse.

CommSqn was a great change for us. After all the useless duties we had been given, it was a relief to have a place to really do some work. The squadron had a variety of aircraft, used to transport personnel, usually high-ranking officers and other VIPs, from here to there. The aircraft were not military, but rather were civilian aircraft with RCAF markings. How these came to be in the RCAF is a story I don't know. They had all been equipped with full communications gear and served their purpose well. I was assigned to an old Grumman Goose. This was an amphibious aircraft and was usually on the water. My first assignment was to replace a defective trailing aerial. While working, I dropped one of my tools, a small item called, of all things, a tool cable stripping. To all intents and purposes, it was a small button hook, with the inside of the hook sharpened. It was designed and used to strip insulation off multi-conductor cables. (These cables were quite common in those days in civilian aircraft, and then during the war in service aircraft as well. They have now been superceded by individual wires, which can be traced for faults and problems more easily.) Well, I dropped this tiny tool, and it slid into the water and settled down in about six inches of silt on the bottom, thus promptly disappearing. I thought little of the matter; it was a small tool and probably not worth much. Later, I broke a small file and threw away the pieces. No one had told me that when you work on any watercraft, you tie the tools to your wrist with the Barbours twine included in every RCAF tool kit!

The day of reckoning came. There was to be a tool kit inspection, and of course all of us were short this or that. When the supply clerk saw that I was missing the tool cable stripping and the small file, he immediately made out an E26 repayment voucher, which meant that whatever was on that document would be deducted from my next pay! Though surprised, I wasn't too concerned until I read the E26. I was to pay $1.87 for the crummy cable stripper, and $0.44 for the file, and then the clerk made an error and extended the file to $0.88, so I ended up paying for two! From then on, I NEVER signed anything without reading it fully first. It sounds like a small amount today, but looking at the pay scales, I paid more than a day's wages for a few tools!

Shortly after I started work at CommSqn, I telephoned Es in Montreal and told her of the situation in Ottawa regarding accommodation. What I had would do for the time being, but once she arrived, it would be necessary for her to find us other quarters. She agreed readily, and arrived a few days later. That first evening we had dinner out, saw what we could of the town, and became acquainted with the streetcar and bus system. We also bought all the newspapers for looking at ads for apartments, rooms, and so forth. We were both very young and more than a little naive. That night there were all sorts of weird noises I hadn't noticed before on our Gloucester Street, and the next morning, at breakfast, a little investigating showed that we were living between two houses of ill repute. This made Es's resolve to find other accommodation all the stronger.

After a few weeks of CommSqn we heard through the grapevine that there was to be an active unit moving into the new hangars under the hill. (These hangars were not actually under the hill, but appeared to be so, as they abutted against the hill behind them.) We all paused at whatever we were doing when two flights of brand new Westland Lysanders flew in. They were really something to see. All decked out in camouflage paint, the Lysanders had large fixed-wheel struts to support the little bomb wings. No bombs were on board, of course, but we could imagine, couldn't we? It was a real thrill, because until then we had only worked on or seen at close hand civilian aircraft, and none of them would ever see action. There were a few front-line aircraft in the Test & Development (T&D) Squadron hangar, but this area was strictly out of bounds to us, and the aircraft were whisked off to the end of the runways as soon as they were out of the hangar, well before we could even get a good look at them. I tried to switch to T&D Sqn, but no soap. They were using only RCAF pre-war Permanent Force personnel, and the rest of us weren't sufficiently skilled or experienced for the front-line aircraft. That's what we were told at any rate, but looking at it from the other side, we were working on aircraft that flew the Brass and VIPs all over the country. We were good enough for that, weren't we? It must have been an excuse, or featherbedding or something!

Then came a few breaks from the routine. One night we were on duty watch, a night detail that cleaned up, met late incoming aircraft, and generally did the dirty work that someone with higher rank didn't want to do. A Noorduyn Norseman was due to come in, and rumour had it that First World War ace Billy Bishop was to be on board. We all strained our eyes as the Norseman touched down. A staff car, complete with chauffeur, drove out onto the apron to meet the aircraft. Billy Bishop was indeed on board the Norseman, and we learned that the staff car was there to whisk him off to the Officers' Mess. That was the plan, at any rate. There was just one small hitch: passes had been issued for the chauffeur and liaison officer, but not for Bishop. But then, who in the world would challenge Billy Bishop?

We had a few PPOs (Provisional Pilot Officers; would-be aircrew) who were being kept useful while they awaited course at an Initial Training School. Most were acting as security guards at various locations within the station area. One of these posts was at the junction of the perimeter road and the hangar road. The perimeter road gave access to the rest of the station, and the junction was directly opposite the old station orderly room. The young PPO at this post was really hard-nosed. He would not permit even Billy Bishop to pass without the necessary documentation. He had his orders, "Sir", and there was no swaying him. Finally, he permitted the liaison officer and the chauffeur to pass through to find the Orderly Officer, or the Officer of the Guard, who could change the PPO's orders. Bishop, however, must remain at the guard post with the security guard.

The Officer of the Guard and the Orderly Officer arrived together, and the former started to give the young lad a blast. Bishop inter-

14 The War Years

vened. "Enough," he said. "I'll see you at 1000 hours tomorrow morning in the Commanding Officer's office, airman!" and he was on his way. We all felt sorry for the kid.

The next day was a beautiful one; spring was in the air. Four of us from CommSqn were detailed to act as escorts for trials at the orderly room and, sure enough, I was in the pair that was to escort the young kid from the previous night. At about 0955 hours, in stomped Billy Bishop, and, about 15 seconds later, in came the Station Warrant Officer (SWO), and they both headed for the CO's office. After a few minutes the SWO reappeared, directed us exactly how we were expected to escort in the PPO, and told us to look smart. He grunted the necessary commands: "Left, right, left, right, HUT", and we were in front of the CO's desk. "HUT" again, and the PPO stepped forward and was directly in front of the CO, with the SWO very close behind him. (In the good ole days long before, an enlisted man charged with some minor offence had jumped over the desk and, before the escort or SWO could stop him, had assaulted the trial officer. Since then, tradition had it that the SWO should be directly behind the accused, ready for just such an emergency!)

The charge was read: "AC2 so and so, while on guard duty, did willfully prevent Air Commodore W. Bishop from leaving the hangar area, even though he was attended by a liaison officer who was in possession of the necessary documentation for his own exit, and who vouched for the Air Commodore, on such and such a day, at such and such a time. How do you plead—guilty or not guilty?"

"Guilty, Sir!" said the PPO.

Suddenly Bishop stepped forward and put his hand on the kid's shoulder. As the SWO stepped back, Bishop said something like: "You, young man, at least know what an order is, and you obey it to the letter—not like the blasted idiots in the orderly room here, who make out passes for all and sundry to pass your guard point and neglect to make one out for the person those people are attending. Son, you're headed for an ITS on the next draft. I'm certain you are aircrew material, and that you will do well."

The case was dismissed and all charges were dropped. The PPO's slate was clean, so he was very relieved. He left the station with a draft going out the following day, about six weeks before he could normally have expected to go. I never did trace that kid, nor do I remember his name, but it would have been interesting to see how he made out, both at ITS and overseas, if he made it. If not for Bishop, the case could easily have ended the PPO's career then and there.

A week or so later the Regiment de Hull moved in to take over guard duty from the PPOs, who in turn were placed on hangar duty. The PPOs enjoyed the hangar duty much more and were able to learn something about aircraft, too. The change in guard brought about a few incidents I recall with considerable amusement even today.

We were again on duty watch. Our work was over, but as no transport was readily available, the group of us went for a walk around the perimeter road. When we arrived at the base of the hill where the new hangars were, the most marvellously delicious smells wafted over to us. Following our noses, we found the smells to be coming from one of a series of huts that had recently been taken over by the Regiment de Hull. The hut in question, of course, was their Mess Hall (they called it the cookhouse).

Now, military cooks are the same the world over; praise them and you have a certain friend for life! Hunger lent us gifted tongues for flattery, and we were soon seated at a board table which had been scrubbed clean with lye soap, with bowls of bean soup, home-made bread, and baked beans sitting before us. Never have beans, soup, and bread tasted so good! Without warning, there was a commotion outside, someone yelled, and there was a rifle shot, followed by three more shots in quick succession. We ran out of the cookhouse to see the CO's staff car, with the CO at the wheel, stopped in the middle of the road. Steam spouted from under the car's hood, and a rather belligerent lance corporal of the Regiment de Hull was holding the CO at bay with his rifle. He was saying something like: "I tell you to stop or I shoot; you no stop, so I shoot. You get out of car, I shoot again." All this in rapid, mixed French and English, but the meaning was by no means lost; it was quite clear!

The Orderly Officer arrived with the Officer of the Guard, and together they convinced the irate lance corporal that he had perhaps misunderstood his orders. The CO and/or his delegate, the Station Adjutant, were the persons who signed his orders and any passes to permit people past his post. So, as he or his delegate signed the passes, they did not need them, did they? Grudgingly, the lance corporal agreed to this interpretation of the orders, and the CO moved on. From then on, the guards recognized and allowed passage to the CO, and the CO had considerably more respect for the guards than heretofore.

Another guard incident comes to mind, one which happened while Es and I were at the station theatre. The Photographic Section offices were in the theatre, which was, by the standards of the day, well secured. All Mapping and Photographic Section records were kept there, and they were also doing classified work, perfecting the camera obscura system. Service personnel and their dependents could view current movies in the theatre for a fraction of the downtown prices, and it was usually a pleasant social evening, as well, for we could use the dry and wet canteens. (The dry canteen sold soft drinks, chocolate bars, etc; the wet canteen sold only beer, and was more or less a tavern.) Such an evening would also provide an opportunity for the wives of servicemen to get some idea of what the station looked like.

On this particular evening, LACs Sand and Toope and their wives accompanied Es and me to the station theatre to see a current movie. I can't for the life of me remember what it was, but I do remember that Es attempted a short cut, off the walk and across the grass. She was stopped cold by a guard with a cocked, loaded rifle. That was one experience neither of us will ever forget.

By that time we were all six-month veterans(!) of the RCAF, and the AC2s were reclassified AC1s. Those few of us who were AC1s were reclassified LACs. Reclassification was almost automatic if you had committed no crimes and received a favourable report from your NCO in command. Among other privileges, the reclassification entitled one to a small pay increment, which was always welcome (no less than a raise is today!).

Es and I were no longer living in the temporary quarters I had obtained on arrival in Ottawa. As the living conditions and neighbourhood of that lodging left something to be desired, Es soon found us other accommodation. She spent many hours poring over the local papers for an apartment. We wanted a furnished place, but these were extremely hard to find and were priced well beyond the reach of our limited finances. She finally found an unfurnished apartment in New Edinborough, and we got a complete houseful of furniture from one of the local stores for a nominal sum, with the balance on the never-never plan.

The New Edinborough apartment was ideal for us. It was part of a small building that was mainly used as a drugstore. The landlord had an apartment on one side of the store and we had the ground floor apartment on the other side, around the corner. A pair of gentlemen had the apartment above ours. It was, we thought, a good deal, and we were quickly moved in and established.

In those days the milkman delivered not only the milk, but also table cream for coffee, whipping cream for desserts, eggs, and orange and tomato juice. Our monthly bill for these commodities was about three dollars. We dealt with a local butcher shop, and did the rest of our shopping at a Dominion Store that was less than half a block away. After about a month we were considered regulars by both of these establishments, and were offered the use of their end-of-the-month plan, similar to that the milkman offered. Strangely enough, our total grocery bill, including the butcher, the baker, and the milkman, never exceeded the amount we had budgeted. Despite the food bill, rent, furniture payments, transportation, the occasional dinner out, and every now and then a movie, we managed quite well on my LAC's wages.

The two gentlemen who lived in the apartment above us had a housekeeper in every day, and she gave the inexperienced Es some advice on budgeting, cooking, and that sort of thing. The only problem was that neither of them knew what sort of food I favoured. Thus far in our married lives, Es had not had the occasion to cook for me, as we had eaten either at a restaurant or at the house on Gloucester Street. One day I came home to a stew. Well, stew is great for those who like it, but in my time in the Army I had seen enough stew for a lifetime. Though I could eat it, I wouldn't unless I really had to.

"What's this, STEW?"

Regardless of the fancy names one might give it, stew is stew. When I got home that night and saw what Es had prepared for our dinner, we suddenly decided to eat out. It wasn't in the budget, but we ate out anyway!

Then there were the peculiar noises we heard at night and sometimes in the early morning. The fellows upstairs complained to the landlord about us making the weird noises, and when we complained about them, Mr. Evers, the landlord, realized there was a mystery. Investigation uncovered a sewer rat problem. Somehow they had worked their way between the walls and into the ceilings and floors. Because the building was shared by a drugstore, the Department of Health demanded that the matter be cleared up immediately. An agency was brought in; they first tried using weasels to chase out the rats, but when that didn't work, they finally had the place fumigated. That worked, but it meant that we had to move out of our apartment for a few days. Fortunately, Mr. Evers picked up the tab, for both accommodation and meals. Es and I weren't broke, but we were close to the edge in those days; those few extra dollars would have been beyond our financial capability.

Back at the base, we had come to learn what a Trade Board was all about. Group C tradesmen were not permitted to sign out (or declare serviceable) an aircraft. Their work had to be checked by someone with Group B or Group A qualifications. This always presented something of a bind. Mind you, I don't believe anyone ever found anything wrong, but much time was lost while the work was double-checked, and the higher tradesman was off his job while he was checking yours. The idea was to try to improve your own trades grouping so this wouldn't be necessary. The Trade Board sat at regular intervals, twice a year, I believe, to examine each individual who applied for higher qualification. You need never apply, but then you would never get any higher pay. This applied to many other trades, as well. Some people made the higher grouping, and some didn't. The recommendation of one's NCO in command helped if someone was a borderline case.

A few of us from CommSqn were transferred to the new unit on the station, the SAC (School of Army Co-operation). This was an active unit, established across the field from CommSqn and T&D with a squadron of new Westland Lysanders. The new hangars amazed us. Like the aircraft they sheltered, the hangars were the latest in every respect. The shops, battery rooms, dope shops, engine shops, supply rooms, offices, and unit orderly room were all very well appointed, and put the station orderly room to shame. It was our guess that if war had not broken out, this area would have been the station headquarters and CommSqn hangars. The hangar doors were the overhead type with chain hoists, and provisions had even been made to have them operated by electric motor. The heavy doors at the CommSqn hangar slid horizontally on tracks and were operated by manpower.

At SAC we were at last able to get our first view of the war; we finally had the feeling that we were contributing more directly to the war effort. That was why we had joined up, wasn't it? Air gunners and pilots were gradually posted in, ready for training by SAC. The Officer Commanding SAC (Officer Commanding, or OC, was not to be confused with the CO, Commanding Officer. The OC commanded a unit, while the CO commanded a station.) was Wing Commander VanVince, and he was determined that he and all the men under him would do their very best. "The aircraft," he announced, "will be ready, and on the line, serviced, every morning, come hail, sleet, snow, rain, shine, or whatever."

One of the OC's projects was communication between the aircraft and a control truck, which could be moved from runway to runway depending on which was in use. Given today's technologies and frequencies, it would have been a piece of cake, but with the limited technology of the day, the few frequencies allotted to us, and the equipment with which we were supplied, it was a completely different story. The RAF gear we were to work with was a TR9D. Its maximum output was about five watts, and it was to operate AM. It was designed to work with a trailing aerial, and the frequency we were allotted meant that the aerial would have to be about 85 feet long. There was no matching network in the equipment, so one had to be devised, to be operated with a whip antennae mounted on the rear bumper of the truck. Well, a group of us tried and tried to get that thing working, but there was no way we could bring it even close to the quality needed to satisfy the OC. T&D came over from across the runways, but they had no better luck than we did. In desperation, the OC called in the National Research Council, who had a laboratory just down the road from the station. After a few weeks of trial and error, they had accomplished no more than we had. In the long run, we got an E for effort, and not a great deal more!

Parades and inspections had quickly become a commonplace for us. On one occasion, I stood next to an airman who was a trifle hung over. Though he was clean and shaven and his clothes were properly pressed, he somehow looked dishevelled. I'm certain you know the type. Well, the CO was doing the inspection that morning with the OC, and the SWO was a pace behind, ready to note the names of offenders. The CO looked this airman over very carefully, and in the roaring voice that had brought him the nickname Bull, shouted, "Did you shave this morning, airman?"

"Yes, Sir!"

The Bull then muttered, "Issue blades, I presume." The inference was that the airman was still using the six issue blades handed out at Manning Depot, and that it was time to buy some new ones. Later in the same inspection, the Bull stood right behind another airman, and in an ear-splitting roar demanded, "Am I hurting you, airman?"

The answer was swift and automatic: "No, Sir!"

"Strange," muttered the Bull, "I'm standing on your hair!" I might mention that when the Bull muttered, it could probably be heard at the Governor General's residence a few miles distant from our parade square!

Early that spring (or late winter, whichever you prefer) we were on "street-lining" in Ottawa for the funeral of the late Governor General, Lord Tweedsmuir. That was my second episode of street-lining. The first was in Montreal for the visit of King George V and Queen Mary, while I was with the Army.

With the approach of summer, we were to start wearing our summer uniforms. The RCAF's summer drill uniforms were of a material similar to denim, though of course it was a light khaki in colour. The uniform felt like a suit of armour and looked terrible. It wouldn't hold a press; the moment you put on your clean uniform, it looked like you had slept in it. In the Army I had learned (from the experts) how to make this uniform soft, supple, and able to hold a press, for a few hours, at least. The procedure was not classified, but appeared to be unknown in the RCAF. It was quite simple: the entire uniform was soaked for about three hours in a mild javel water solution, then scrubbed with lye soap and a very stiff bristle brush. Then it was machine-washed. The only pause between these steps was a thorough rinse, but the drill must not be dried. After the machine-washing the drill was allowed to dry naturally in free air. The final step was to send the uniform to the dry cleaners. When it came back, it was soft and quite wearable. It even looked good! I had a pair of Army issue short trousers that had been through this procedure, and they were generally admired. When I ran my summer drill through the process, it stood out on parade. Of course, everyone wanted to find out how I had done it. One of the boys set up a small business processing the uniforms for the others. He didn't make a bundle, but he did prosper!

A pair of RAF liaison NCOs were attached to SAC, an F/S Emas and a Cpl Hand. They had been posted in on the understanding that we would be using RAF wireless gear in our aircraft, gear in which they were well versed. But from Day One, it was quite obvious that the only RAF radio gear we would use was that miserable TR9D in the aerodrome control truck! Of course, we would have to use the RAF's Plug 58 and Socket 29. These plugs and sockets were used in all RAF and RCAF aircraft and headsets. A standard in all aircraft used on the line in Britain, the plugs and sockets were extremely durable, so they became a wartime standard in Canada as well. The two RAF NCOs could operate their radios with extreme skill and thoroughly knew the gear they were trained on, but they weren't radio men as we understood the term—a step away from their own equipment, and they were lost! The RAF used a system similar to that which the USAF uses today, known as the black-box method. Whenever something went wrong that a changed module, tube, or plug-in part couldn't fix, the equipment was sent to the depot for repair, and replacement equipment was used. But even though the two RAF men were nearly helpless with broken equipment, they did give us a great deal of encouragement, and we needed that.

F/S Emas was a rather corpulent man of about 35. He was away from 'ome and family and wasn't too happy about it. Being away from England wasn't anything new to Chieffie, but to be away from his family was another thing. They had been with him in Singapore, India, and Palestine, but now he had left them to face the flak in England, where all the bother was, while he was living off the fat of the Canadian land. He worried about them almost continuously, but when we were able to divert him for a brief while he could be fascinating. He knew all the dialects from the countries he had been in and he could tell innumerable stories about his experiences in far-away lands. It was a pleasure to hear him talk of his travels and the many experiences of his career.

Cpl Hand was a diminutive cockney type, who could and did make himself quite at 'ome anywhere he happened to be. Comfortable in almost every situation, he knew how to adjust. In Canada, and at SAC, he did just that.

Chieffie Emas was the sort of person who didn't drink beer, he absorbed it! I didn't attend too many of his long vigils at the tavern in the Chateau Laurier, but one day he twisted my arm. I made an excuse at home and accompanied him and the boys to the Chateau. We were at a table for eight, and the first round, he said, was on the Chieffie. From his pocket he then pulled 14 shillings (in Canada?), which he divided into three piles, one of three, one of four, and one of seven.

"This," he said, "is a game of skill. Two people play. Each draws as many shillings as he likes from the table in turn, from any one pile at a time. You can draw from any pile you wish; it doesn't have to be the same pile as the other person drew from. The person who must draw the last coin from the table loses. The draws are in succession." He obviously knew the game quite well, but he played a sample game with each of us and was cagey enough to let the occasional party win. He then said he would take us on one at a time, for the drinks.

You can guess what happened. He won hands down! After accumulating about five beers, he paused to mention that the game was called Chinese Pyramids and that it had been taught to him in Inja! by a bloke who had learned it in Hong Kong. The evening wore on. I was to be either seventh or eighth to play against Chieffie, and while waiting I tried desperately to remember what my high school mathematics teacher, Mr. Gulliver, had taught me about combinations and permutations. I remembered Mr. Gulliver well, because I had enjoyed the subject and the way he taught it. He was a dedicated teacher who really knew the art of teaching, and almost all of his work stuck with me.

By the time my turn came I thought I had it worked out. Beezie Sand wasn't the world's best math type and he had failed miserably in his attempt to outplay the Chieffie. Cliffe Toope hadn't fared much better, and then it was my turn. Chieffie generously offered me first draw, which I refused. Praise be to Mr. Gulliver, it worked! I remembered what he had taught me, and I won! I'll never forget that evening. My reference to Mr. Gulliver is not made in jest. He was my first experience of a dedicated and devoted teacher, and there are, to my certain knowledge, too few of these people left.

Westland Lysander 438 during overhaul at RCAF Station Rockcliffe, Ontario, 1940.

I took Chieffie on again later that night for five more games—no prize, just games—and by the end of the last one he grudgingly admitted that I understood the game. We parted later that night, still the best of friends. A few days later he was off—over 'ome, back to the people and the life he really loved.

At SAC everyone working in the hangar was ordered to wear hangar boots. Issued by supply, they were felt boots with heavy felt soles, similar to some extent to the inner boots obtained with snowmobile boots or mukluks today. I imagine they served their purpose well in peacetime, when time was less important and when fabric-covered aircraft were the rule rather than the exception. They were the only boots permitted on the light green area of the hangar floor, the main area. Regular boots, overshoes, and shoes could be worn on the brown walking areas, outlined in red. The entire floor was kept at a gleaming shine, but if possible, the light green area was even shinier. Whenever an aircraft was pushed into the hangar, its tracks (if it dared to make any tracks at all) were mopped up immediately, and the area was swiftly repolished. A drip tray was placed under the aircraft's engine nacelle to catch any drops of oil or coolant. The wheels of the aircraft were placed on small squares of material so as not to damage the floor, or the paint, or the shine, or whatever. A month or so before I left SAC the hangar boots were withdrawn, and I never ever heard of them again during my entire career in the RCAF. The floors of SAC still shone, despite the loss of the boots, because the fitters and riggers (aero engine and air frame mechanics) worked very hard to keep the place immaculate. SAC was always a showplace, and W/C VanVince never had cause to be ashamed of the appearance of the school he had established and loved.

Es and I didn't own a car, but we never noticed the lack of it, nor did we envy those airmen who had one. Public transportation was adequate for our needs, and of course we were young, we had feet, and we could walk. One of the wireless operators, LAC Caron, had a coupe with a rumble seat. He decided to go home on leave once, and as it was too far for him to drive on rationed gas, he planned to go by train. He left the coupe with me for safekeeping, and told me to use it as though it were my own. Well, it sat in our side driveway for a week, because I saw no reason to use it. Then my sister and a mutual girlfriend of ours came to Ottawa for a visit. The four of us drove

Westland Lysanders "peeling off".

about Ottawa in comfort and style, as Es and I showed the visitors the sights and the places we had discovered. I even drove them down to the hangar line, though I was promptly ordered off. (I left without argument, which would be most uncharacteristic of me today!) We were able to see a lot of the town, so the car was a real asset. When LAC Caron returned, I told him how we had used the car to drive all around the town, and he appeared quite upset that I hadn't used it even more.

Es and I had made friends with a few LAC air gunners attached to SAC as trainees. Three of them were RAF, and we came to know them quite well, often having them over for dinner at our apartment. Once they were in a publicity photograph in the rotogravure insert section of one of the local newspapers. Then one day they were promoted and shipped overseas. We heard through the grapevine that they never made it; their convoy received a hit and they were among the casualties. That sort of thing is never easy to take, war or no war.

At about that time we received our Stinson 105s. These aircraft were supposed to be used to give our pilots more flying time. They filled their purpose, but these little civilian aircraft were mere toys, never intended for the day-in, day-out flying they were subjected to at SAC. They died their natural deaths rather early but with dignity, and no one could ever say they hadn't done their duty.

Shortly after the arrival of the Stinsons, we received a few Grumman Goblins from the USA. The Goblins were bi-planes, intended for aircraft carrier service. Like the Lysanders, they had an exceedingly low stall speed, but they didn't come equipped with radio gear. This, then, was to be my first real technical chore. My first installation job was detailed to me by the Signals Officer, F/O Hood. He had been a WOEM, who had somehow managed to get on an RCAF pilot's course and had graduated, I think as a sergeant pilot. When war was declared he was commissioned, and he then served with SAC as both a pilot and the officer in charge of the wireless section.

It must be realized that WOEM's handled a multitude of trades. They were wireless mechanics who looked after both ground and airborne equipment. They were wireless operators, airborne and ground, who could operate their equipment with voice or Morse. They were aircraft electricians, who looked after the electrical services of the aircraft, including not only the lighting system, but all other electrical functions as well—the electrical starters, the generators, the bomb release equipment, and so on. In early 1940 new trades were developed. Wireless operators came into being, and aircraft electricians formed a new trade, but neither of those categories were removed from the WOEM's duties until 1941. With today's sophisticated equipment, the amalgamation of just the air and ground equipment is more than any one technician can handle (at least, in the eyes of the military).

A new piece of radio equipment had just been shipped in, the ATR5. (Translation: Airborne Transmitter/Receiver, Type 5. This type was a 12-volt version, while Type 8 was a 24-volt version.) The ATR5 was a two-channel, fixed frequency, crystal controlled transmitter/receiver, complete with intercommunication so the pilot could talk with anyone in the rear seat. A new device, the electronic fine tune, was very effective, as it allowed the crystals which kept the transmitter and receiver on frequency to be less exact, and thus they were easier and less expensive to produce. This new gear seemed to be exactly what was needed for the Goblins. The only problem was that the ATR5s I would be using were Canadian, whereas the Goblins were American. The American radio gear was built in two pieces, with the motor generator separately mounted, so the tray built in to the aircraft to hold the light second piece was not very sturdy. The Canadian gear was a one-piece unit, and the built-in tray looked too flimsy to hold it. The location was ideal, but weight was a problem. The Signals Officer contacted the eggheads, who looked the deal over, diddled with their slide rules and micrometers, and decided the tray was sufficiently strong to handle the stress. With the green light for the installation, I started on the job. It wasn't all that difficult a task, and in a few days the job was completed and ground-checked.

I reported to F/O Hood, the Signals Officer, that the installation had been completed and just needed his approval, as I had signed the aircraft out as serviceable insofar as wireless was concerned. The corporal in charge was a Group A WOEM and he had countersigned my Group C signature. (Signing an L14 was a ritual. In effect, it was an aircraft log, containing the signatures of all the tradesmen who certified that the aircraft was serviceable or unserviceable in each of the various trades. The pilot could sign out an aircraft even if was unserviceable in one trade, but it was then his responsibility. When he returned from a flight, he signed the log himself, designating any unserviceabilities that would need to be checked.) Almost before the report was out of my mouth, Hood was out of his office and going down to the hangar floor to look the installation over. A glance at the L14 confirmed that the aircraft was serviceable in the other necessary trades, so Hood signed out the Goblin. The installation looked okay, he said, but he wanted to test it in flight.

Now, I had no arguments with his flying the Goblin, but as he crossed the floor on his way to the locker room, he shouted to me to don a suit, grab a chute, and climb into the rear seat. I was not all that fond of flying, so I was quick to object to Hood's plan, but he put it to me very succinctly: "You did the installation and you signed the L14, so now you'll fly in the thing to prove your signature is good!" Unable to argue with his logic, I borrowed the necessary kit and climbed aboard.

We had been airborne for about ten minutes when Hood casually mentioned that it was his first flight in a Goblin. That didn't make me feel too great (Great! Hell, I was scared stiff!), but I couldn't and didn't say a word. A moment later he said he was going to give the aircraft and the radio installation a short test, by performing a little dive. I had no way of knowing how high we were or at what speed we were flying when he went into that dive, but suddenly, as we pulled out of the dive proper, the radio was in my lap, tray and all. The eggheads had been right—the tray was indeed strong enough—but the slide mountings that held the tray to the airframe obviously were not! Other than the severing of the cable that connecting the radio to the aircraft wiring, there appeared to be only superficial damage to the equipment. The intercom still worked, so I promptly told Hood what had happened, and he headed back toward the station.

Then Hood discovered that the hydraulic system which lowered the wheels was inoperative. He told me how to use the manual system beside my seat, but the lever was bent slightly, so that idea was out as well. So there we were, with a radio that didn't work and an aircraft which couldn't get its wheels down. The situation seemed grim to me, and my confidence didn't improve when Hood climbed to a reasonable height and ordered me to bail out.

"What will you do?" I asked.

"I'm responsible for this aircraft, and I'm going to ride it down," he replied. "Now bail out!"

Choosing what seemed the lesser of two dangers, I told him that the radio had jammed between me and the housing, so I couldn't get

"Hello!
No wheels?"

out (not true, but a little white lie). Anyway, I said, I'd rather trust him that some parachute rigger I didn't know. If he didn't mind, I'd prefer to stick with him.

Hood seemed pleased. He wasted no time descending to what I considered a very low altitude. After he had made a few passes at the control tower, we saw the fire trucks and crash tenders roaring toward the runway in use. Hood was ready for them, and he began to descend for the landing. There was still a fair-sized snowbank on either side of the runway, and Hood told me he was going to try to land on one of them to cushion the shock. My heart in my mouth, I prepared myself for a crash.

It was the smoothest landing I had ever experienced in the RCAF. Hood pulled the nose up so that not even a prop was bent as the aircraft slid to a stop. On our walk back to the hangar, Hood told me that because the Goblin had been designed for carrier service, the bellies were made of steel. They were really quite safe for landing without the use of wheels, even on grass, as long as the pilot kept the aircraft's nose up. Hood had apparently read the handbook extensively and knew a great deal about the Goblin.

Needless to say, the tray supports on all the Goblins were reinforced before any more radios were installed. Protectors were laced over the cables which served the landing gear systems. No doubt the eggheads rationalized away the problems we encountered on our flight by saying we had asked them to certify only the tray, not the supports, thus saving themselves any embarrassment or recrimination.

W/C VanVince, the OC of SAC, had many worthwhile ideas that were well ahead of their time, witness the unsuccessful attempt to perfect a communication control truck. Another example involves our horizontal plotting boards. These were basically enlarged maps of the station and the tactical area used by SAC, with houses, roads, bridges, and so forth clearly marked in map language. We also had vertical boards indicating terrain heights, but it still required considerable imagination to picture the territory the two types of boards represented. The W/C's idea was to redesign the horizontal boards so they would show the ground contours. We were to make a sort of sand box with a 20-by-20 foot perimeter. Chicken wire was to be shaped to form the scaled-down contours of the map area, and the wire would then be covered with cloth. For rigidity, the cloth would be doped, and then painted in colours as much like the real landscape as possible. Small models of houses, trees, and so on would represent those actually on the terrain and make the entire affair realistic. (A good many model train enthusiasts of today use a similar system to make a "landscape" for their hobby.) The whole thing was to be to scale, of course, and would have movable trucks, tanks, and so forth. It would thus give pilots and observers an excellent idea of what to look for during flights and what developments to report back to base.

For an early wartime effort, the idea appeared quite frivolous, but the W/C usually got what he wanted and this was no exception. We had no sooner put the finishing touches on our new plotting box than the W/C let us in on a modification. To increase the realism, he wanted us to devise an electro-magnetic system for moving about the trucks and armour. Either he hadn't thought of this when he originally designed the box or he had neglected to place us in his full confidence. Whatever the situation, it was too late to incorporate this new idea.

Had we known, we could have used copper mesh as the base rather than chicken wire. I must admit that I'm glad we weren't told earlier, because that control system would have been a real headache, opening the door to more complexities than we were ready for at the time. It would have been possible, of course, had we used copper mesh instead of chicken wire, and the difference in price at that time would have been negligible. In any case, we weren't told in time, and the subject was closed. To the surprise of many of us, the finished plotting box proved to be a valuable training aid.

A portion of the school, including myself, suddenly went off to Malton for an exercise. At the time, we gave little thought to the reasoning behind our brief trip. After we had been back at Rockcliffe for a week or so, we were sent to Petawawa for a few weeks of intensive exercise with the Royal Canadian Horse Artillery, my old outfit, returning to Rockcliffe as soon as the exercises were over. In early March of 1941 some of the people who had been with SAC since its inception were posted out. We all realized that SAC

Bezie Sand and unknown sergeant check out an AR4.

was beginning to contribute something to the war effort. We were experienced with a good variety of things by this time, including the training of gunners, pilots, and observers on the wireless equipment. (Some of those we had trained had already appeared on casualty lists from overseas; their war had been short.) We had worked with the new AT1/AR2 12-volt transmitter-receiver combinations. We had tested and used and loved the rugged AR4 battery-operated ground receivers and had helped to install some of the newest, high-power, ground transmitters at the station transmitter site. This ground transmitter, the AT3 (Air Transportable Transmitter Mark 3), was a 500-watt A.M. transmitter with a novel remote control system. Some of these transmitters are still in use today and continue to operate very efficiently. (Those used today are not used by the RCAF, but rather by civilian organizations who recognized the worth of the transmitters and purchased them from war surplus.)

Out of the blue, I received a posting to Bela Bela in British Columbia. It turned out to be a prank engineered by one of the unit's jokers, but it wasn't long before a real posting came in. I was to go to No. 3 Bombing and Gunnery School at Macdonald, Manitoba. Es and I promptly sold most of what furniture we owned and returned the furniture we had obtained on the never never plan. She headed for Montreal to stay with her parents until I could find accommodation out West, if and when I found out how long I was going to be there. As it was wartime, the RCAF was not going to pay her way out, nor pay for the movement of her necessary effects. That would be my financial problem. As well, I would have to determine just what accommodation and transportation would cost in the nearest town to Macdonald to see if I could afford to live out. There were a lot of things to consider when you lived on an LAC's pay, particularly when you were moving to unknown territory and it was your first experience, so to speak, of going away from home. After all, Ottawa and Montreal were practically next door to one another, but not so Macdonald, Manitoba. That was a horse of a different colour!

3

No. 3 Bombing & Gunnery School Macdonald, Manitoba March 1941 - October 1944

WHAT WAS A B&G SCHOOL, and where in Canada was Macdonald, Manitoba? That was the question of the day. No one at SAC had so much as heard of the place, let alone knew where it was. I finally learned from a helpful clerk at the Ottawa railway station that Macdonald was a few miles north of Portage la Prairie, which was about fifty miles west of Winnipeg. The only way to get there was to take the train to Portage la Prairie and then climb aboard a milk-run bus for the last stage of the journey. The rail station at Macdonald was for freight (grain) only. What was a B&G School? The answer to that question would have to wait until I arrived in Macdonald; everyone I asked at Rockcliffe was willing to take a guess, but no one knew for sure. All that was certain was that it was part of the British Commonwealth Air Training Plan (BCATP). There was a critical need to staff these units as rapidly as possible, so Canada could start turning out qualified aircrew to man the aircraft being manufactured throughout the Commonwealth for the defence of Britain.

I had been reclassified as an LAC by this time and, having passed at least one Trade Board, was a Group B tradesman. Hence, I was permitted to sign out aircraft as serviceable and was considered of some value to a wireless section. Moreover, I knew how to install and service a wide variety of RCAF radio equipment. We had been technically relieved of the "O" in the WOEM designation of our trade by this time, as official wireless operators were increasing in number, but knowledge of operating procedures was still a requirement for us in the eyes of the Trade Board. As well, we were (again, technically) relieved of the "E" of WOEM, for there were now a quantity of aircraft electricians trained specifically to look after all electrical systems and batteries in the aircraft. Nonetheless, the "E" stayed in our trade specifications. I had hopes that when I arrived in Macdonald, I could sit before the earliest Trade Board to get my Group A designation, as well as possibly earning my corporal's stripes.

On the train going west I met a corporal air frame mechanic, who was headed for a B&GS at Paulson, Manitoba, well north of Macdonald. He knew something of the BCATP, and was happy to pass this information along. Apparently, most B&G Schools used Avro Ansons for navigation training, bomb-aiming, and transport. At Macdonald I would find Fairey Battles, single-engined, low-wing monoplanes with in-line, glycol-cooled Rolls Royce engines. They had free guns (that is, without turrets), but turret modifications were said to be in the works. Furthermore, a good many of the aircraft were war veterans, with battle scars still visible. Although most of the Battles were still camouflaged, a number had been repainted in the black and yellow "hornet" scheme used for drogue tows to clearly distinguish them from gunnery aircraft. There was quite a mystique surrounding drogueing. The drogue was a 20- or 30-foot cloth sleeve about two feet in diameter, and was towed on a steel cable, which was winch-operated from the belly of the aircraft. The drogue was fired on with painted bullets by the gunnery aircraft. Some of the colour came off when it hit the drogue, and thus the gunner's score could be determined. The coloured marks were circled with black as they were counted, and thereafter ignored. When one drogue had been fired on by a complete flight of aircraft, it was discarded by the release of a second drogue down the cable. It all sounded very simple, but I was later to find out that the process was more difficult than it appeared.

The corporal's descriptions were all very interesting, but where did radios come into the picture? He had an answer for that, as well. As a safety precaution, the drogue aircraft were to be radio-equipped. These aircraft were (almost) in the line of fire, and they were also the aircraft up in the air for the longest period. A shortage of equipment had prevented all drogue aircraft from being radio-equipped.

Arriving at Portage, I was relieved to find that the anticipated bus journey would not be necessary, as an RCAF transport was waiting for me when I debarked. The transport took me immediately to the No. 3 B&GS station orderly room, where I signed in and was allotted a bed in the barracks. A word about these: the barracks at No. 3 B&GS were identical to those in a good many BCATP stations. One-storey H-huts, they were coal-heated, which meant that men from W&B (Works and Buildings) periodically refilled the hoppers that automatically fed the coal to the furnaces. The furnaces were efficient for the time, but they did have the occasional tendency to belch smoke. Each side of the H-hut was permitted one furnace. In the centre of the hut was a communal washroom, and at the top and bottom of each leg was a corporal's room. Rows of double-decker bunk beds lined the rest of each leg, with lockers above the bunks for one's kit. Some lucky fellows managed to obtain vertical lockers as well, allowing them the luxury of keeping their uniforms looking pressed and respectable. If clothes were simply hung beneath the overhead lockers, dust from the furnace quickly seeped its way into every fold and corner. (Plastic sleeves for covering clothes were unheard of in those days.) The design of the H-hut was not very glamorous, but it served its purpose well. As soon as I had found my assigned bunk and put my name tag at its foot, I followed the crowd to the mess for lunch.

Lunch was the heavy meal of the day at a BCATP station, the meat-potatoes-vegetables-gravy meal. It was served on crockery plates and cups, cafeteria-style, all you could eat (but don't dare waste any), and the food was excellent. There was always a salad bar, and all the usual beverages were available. Staff and trainees all ate in the same mess hall, which promoted good relations and avoided discrimination (and I use here a very modern word) of any kind. The trainees were from anywhere and everywhere—Canadians, British, New Zealanders, and Australians, all sizes, shapes, and colours. All were dedicated to the task before them, a dedication that had been instilled in these young aircrew at Initial Training School. Some, of course, thought themselves better than the mechanics who kept their aircraft serviced, but a week or so at the school and they quickly realized that their lives depended on those greasy slobs they were occasionally forced to sit beside in the mess. Fellow mechanics told me it usually took just a week for the aircrew's snobbishness to vanish. Then it was just a matter of an evening or so at the wet canteen, and everyone was fighting the same war, on the same side, and all was well with the world.

I reported to the wireless section immediately after lunch, and in a small shop I found a worried-looking red-headed flight sergeant, surrounded by a few tables and numerous packing cases crammed with equipment. When I told him who I was, he greeted me with wide open arms. F/S Unit and I were to meet each other regularly throughout our Air Force careers. Now that we are both retired, he as a squadron leader and I as a warrant officer, we still visit each other as often as we can. At this, our initial meeting, his first words were of some wierd new piece of equipment they had, an ATR5. Had I ever heard of it? A Permanent Force NCO, Unit had trained on RAF gear, and I think he was a bit baffled by the Canadian gear. Overjoyed to hear that this "new" equipment was old hat to me, Unit set me to work immediately as together we installed one ATR5 in a drogue Battle. A second ATR5 with a large complement of batteries was then hooked up as a ground station. It took a good many batteries every day to keep the ground ATR5 running. The airborne ATR5s presented no such problem, as the aircraft generator kept the batteries fully charged. The results of this "new" gear were gratifying to Unit and me, and a surprise to all others. Everyone had been used to the limited power of the RAF gear, and was delighted with the excellent range and voice quality of the ATR5.

Engine noise in the background still caused difficulties, until the eggheads at NRC came through with a relatively simple modification that almost eliminated engine noise yet had no appreciable effect on voice quality. We were using carbon microphones similar to those used in telephones and manufactured by the same company. The case of the microphone holder was bakelite (somewhat like modern plastic, but not as durable) and, like a telephone receiver, was screwed together. The NRC modification couldn't have been simpler: the perforated casing over the microphone into which one spoke was to be unscrewed and a small cambric disc inserted between the casing and the face of the microphone. We WOEMs were sceptical, but did a test modification on one of the ATR5s. It worked! The eggheads were useful! Apparently the type of cambric used had a damping effect on the frequency of the noise produced by the engines, but had practically no effect on voice frequencies. This type of cambric, also called oilskin, is akin to the material used by the down-easters on their raincoats. Dosed with some chemical that makes it waterproof, the oilskin nonetheless remains quite flexible.

We installed the modified ATR5s in all the drogue ships. Those Battles for which we didn't have radios were fitted with the ATR5 mounting trays, cables, and remote controls, so that when a radio-equipped ship went u/s (unserviceable), we could simply remove the radio from the u/s ship and install it in one of these aircraft. Thus, a radio-equipped aircraft could be ready for the morning line-up.

The installation process took a few weeks, but was well worth the time, and we all felt much satisfaction in our accomplishment. During those few weeks my documents arrived from SAC and I was able to sit for a Trade Board. With my A Group designation, I was ready for anything. I was also promoted to acting corporal, and those stripes with their accompanying privileges made me feel that I had the world by the tail. My slightly increased pay meant that I would be able to send Es the necessary money for her to join me as soon as I found accommodation.

F/S Unit and a good many of the staff lived in Portage la Prairie. There was a regular bus service to Macdonald, and it was much more efficient than I had originally anticipated. Some of the base staff used a Portage hotels as a boarding house, but this was a little rich for our blood. Es and I wanted a touch more home life than a sterile hotel room could afford. Portage itself was a great little town. A few restaurants and hotels, two theatres, and one main street with dozens of lesser streets running off it—that was Portage. I mustn't forget to mention the school, the hospital, and the jail, and there was also a large railyard, which was a major portion of Portage la Prairie.

Our first landlady in Portage was a certain Mrs. Rand. She rented us a very pleasant room on the second floor of her home. Four other rooms were also rented, one to an army chaplain with a bad stomach, one to an army captain and his very British wife, and two to aircrew trainees and their wives. All the men normally ate at their barracks or the station, myself included, but our wives, of course, had their meals at Mrs. Rand's. The rent for my wife's comfortable room had seemed quite reasonable, but I quickly discovered that I was being charged an extra dollar over and above the agreed amount for every night I spent with my wife at Mrs. Rand's. When I complained, I was told (and not so politely) that this was the way it was and it was not negotiable. All the married types in the house were charged in the same way!

Father Rouse, the chaplain with the bad stomach, had his share of difficulties with Mrs. Rand, too. His health made it necessary for him to visit the facilities frequently. Whenever Mrs. Rand heard him trudging upstairs to the bathroom, she would shout after him, "Flush only once, Father. Remember, water costs money!" Ah yes, this was the house of brotherly love.

We had a small cat which kept Es (and the other young wives) company during the day. I brought home the milk for it, for we knew by this time that Mrs. Rand would have charged us the price of a bottle for saucerful. One winter night Es and I were awakened by the cat's piteous meowing. It was cold outside the warmth of the bed, so cold that the milk in the cat's saucer had frozen over! We turned on a table lamp and set the bowl of frozen milk under it. The milk soon melted, and the cat was able to lap up her long-awaited drink. In the morning, we found the sleeping cat curled about the base of the still-lit lamp. I guess she was cold, too. So much for "heated, comfortable rooms"!

"Heated, comfortable rooms!"

Even during the day the house was often miserably cold for the women. One of the trainee's wives was pregnant and felt the cold a bit more than the others. One day, unable to bear the chill, she plugged in her electric pressing iron, wrapped it in a towel, and popped it under the blankets to warm her feet. Though it was the middle of the day, she was so comfortable that she fell asleep, and, you guessed it, the towel and the sheets were badly scorched. Fortunately, Mrs. Rand was out at the time, and one of the other wives smelled the burning and was able to help the trainee's wife get the mess cleaned up and the room aired out in record time. But what were they to do about the bedsheets? There was nothing for it but to replace them with new ones, purchased from the young wife's scanty savings. They figured that if they had reported the scorching to Mrs. Rand, she would have charged not only double what the sheets were worth, but also an extra fee for the electricity used in scorching them!

Our stay at Mrs. Rand's house was punctuated with problems. Some were perhaps of our own making, but others were certainly not. That first winter in Portage was a cold one, but not as cold as some we have experienced since, and we never again had to go to such lengths to protect ourselves from the cold. A few days after the incident of the cat's milk, the temperature dropped a few degrees lower. Es and I had just returned from the theatre and we found our room a trifle cool, but thought it must just be the chill from the outside still with us. At any rate, we went to bed, but it was still cold. After a short while I looked at our thermometer, and it read below 50 degrees Fahrenheit. In our opinion, that was COLD. Well, Mrs. Rand had retired, so we could do little but bear with it. Es and I each put on a pair of my service-issue long johns (which I had never before found necessary) and added my issue greatcoat to the blankets covering the bed, and with the light left on for the cat, we eventually nodded off to sleep. The next morning all the pipes in the bathroom were frozen, but that didn't phase Mrs. Rand in the least. She knew just where to apply a little heat to get the plumbing working in jig time. She knew all the tricks, but it was our first, and last, winter in her house!

Other landlords and landladies were not necessarily the same, but we had our share of both the unreasonable and the reasonable. Of course, there are those we will never forget for their understanding of our situation.

There was a mock occupation day in Portage one year. I don't recall the exact date, but I do remember the orders that were posted throughout the town. The stores were closed, and all passes were carefully examined by the "occupation forces" during that period. The idea was most effective. In all the towns where this little charade was carried out, the citizens and servicemen came to a much better view of the war and began to realise to a small degree what some of the people of Europe were going through right then. It also had the effect of making things a little easier for those of us in the service. Up till then we had been, to some people, pigeons to be plucked, suckers to be taken to the cleaners whenever possible. This attitude was much rarer after the mock occupation day.

The corporal air frame mechanic I had met on the train coming out to Macdonald had been surprised that I hadn't stayed in the Army and gone on to the guns as I had been offered in December 1939. I didn't understand his attitude until I had spent a few months in Macdonald, watching the continual shift of personnel as some men were posted in and others were posted out. The corporal had been under the natural impression that I, like most of those in the Army, had been with my battery almost from day one and had become an integral part of that unit. The Army unit is normally a fairly static, closely knit one. Not so the RCAF. In the Air Force, personnel are shifted about as the powers-that-be see fit, and individuals are expected to melt quickly into the system. My experiences in the Army, being shifted about from unit to unit as my expertise was required, was how the Air Force treated all their personnel. The Army and Air Force were normally quite different in that respect, but I had never thought much about it till my time in Macdonald.

I had a lot to learn—about life in general, about life in the RCAF, about life in a small town, and, in particular, about life in the RCAF in a small town with a wife! I had a lot to learn about prairie people too. One of the senior NCOs I came to know in W&B was a civilian come flight sergeant, whom I will call Sid. (Work and Buildings personnel, known in peacetime as construction engineers, were the people who looked after the buildings, roads, hangars, PMQs, station electrical systems, fire-fighting, and all general maintenance, even the station heating system, if there was one, which we often doubted!) Sid was a general contractor in civilian life, and he also owned a farm implement store in Portage la Prairie. How he came to be in the RCAF as a flight sergeant, I will never know. With him in W&B were several other civilians he had arranged to bring in, including a sergeant (instant variety) master plumber who was far too old to have been enlisted, but Sid managed it! With Sid as foreman of W&B, the group of them really made the section work. All this activity and energy was despite the efforts of a little engineering officer, whose diploma had hardly dried in its frame.

One afternoon while Sid and I were chatting on the bus returning to Portage, he asked if I would be interested in doing the repairs on some radios that were piling up in his shop. Sid still managed the store during the evenings, but he knew next to nothing about repairing electrical equipment. His regular serviceman had joined the Army, but that didn't stop the repair work from being brought into the shop. All the tools and test equipment I would need were there. I checked with F/S Unit, who voiced no objections provided it did not interfere with my RCAF work. Thus I began to make a few buckshee bucks and at the same time provide Portage with a necessary service. That was PR before the RCAF created an active Public Relations.

Sid's wife was a schoolteacher, and as Sid and I came to know one another, his wife and Es grew to be fast friends. One evening Sid and I finished at the store and left the door unlocked while we waited for our wives to arrive so we could all head off to a show. What looked very much like a derelict came in and started kicking the tires of some of the farm machinery that Sid had for sale. Pointing to one particular piece of equipment, he asked Sid a number of questions—was delivery available to his farm, what sort of service would be available on breakdown, and so forth. When satisfied, he put his hand in the pocket of his tattered overalls and pulled out a roll of bills that would choke a horse. He paid CASH on a bill that involved three or four thousand dollars. That was a lot of money, particularly in those days. I thought it very odd—all that money, and he in tattered clothes. Well, I did say I had a lot to learn, didn't I?

In '41 and '42 Canada was quite short of pilots, but we had a lot of volunteers from the United States who wanted to fly in combat. Of course, a good many, for a number of reasons, were not suitable for service overseas, and these pilots remained in Canada to fly for the B&G and Wireless Schools. They were, I believe, enlisted by contract and received their pay increments by promotions. Some started off as officers, others as sergeant pilots. Needless to say, a few of them were bums, but most were gentlemen indeed, and were a credit and an asset to the RCAF.

I remember the day I was promoted to sergeant and F/S Unit took me to the Sergeants' Mess for lunch. One of the sergeant pilots, a Texan, was the type who was always right while the rest of the world was wrong. That particular sergeant and I had already had a few sessions of words, and I had mentally promised that bird a day of reckoning. Well, on that day I went along to the cloak-room to get rid of my coat and hat and was about to enter the mess proper when a heavy hand attached itself to my shoulder and a loud voice, with the twang of a Texan, roared in my ear, "Who the hell let you in here?" Five years of intensive judo training in the Army tends to instill a certain instinct in a man; I grabbed the wrist attached to the hand and, with some of that drilled-in expertise, flipped the sergeant pilot over my head. He landed flat on his back on the floor of the mess, and in true judo style I placed my foot on his chest without even thinking about it. Tex just lay there; he had obviously been hurt, but whether it was actual physical damage or just a severe blow to his pride, I don't know. After all, Tex was 220 pounds, six and a half feet tall, and a real braggart. He was carted off to hospital for a day or two, but I didn't feel in the least upset, other than some concern that I might have scratched the highly polished mess floor. I was later told that word went out—probably from Tex—"Don't mess with that $i*&! sergeant in the wireless section!" It had been been pure instinct on my part; no one, but no one, places a hand on my

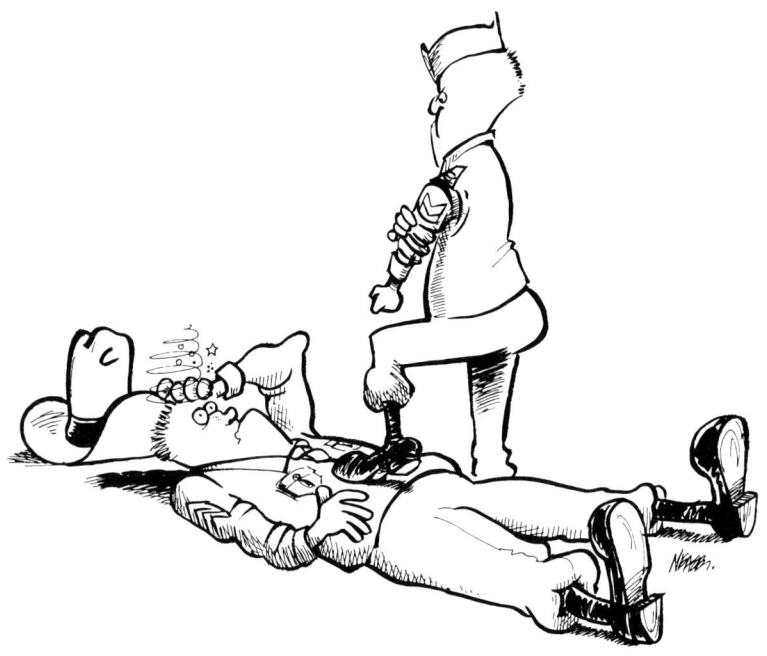

"Defend yourself at all times!"

shoulder from the rear without facing the consequences. It had been drummed into me for five years—*"No one approaches you from behind with other than malice aforethought. Defend yourself!"* I did, I had, and I was glad!

We had a lot of good guys too, and, fortunately, they were definitely in the majority. The officer in charge of the maintenance hangar was F/L Boyd, an American contract pilot. He left much to be desired as far as dress was concerned, but he did know how to fly, and his knowledge of aircraft maintenance was unsurpassed. He could handle the AFMs and the AEMs, and soon had the respect of their senior NCOs as well, and that's all that was needed to get them working at top efficiency. Thanks to Boyd, we had one rather unusual Fairey Battle without an RCAF number. It was lettered JOEB after its creator, Joe Boyd. Assembled from various wrecks, it had a port wing from that wreck, a starboard wing from this one, a prop from the one over there, and an engine from this one here. The engine nacelle was painted with a shark's face, and the white teeth gleamed as hungrily as those of the famed Flying Tigers, leading everyone to think Joe had once been with that team. The whole

F/L Joe Boyd with his JOEB at No. 3 B&G School, Macdonald.

machine was strictly against regulations, but Joe flew it, largely because he knew he shouldn't (but after all, the JOEB didn't officially exist). How he procured gas for it was something else no one could quite figure out, but somehow or other the JOEB was always fuelled up and on the line. Whenever an aircraft went down somewhere, Boyd was in his JOEB and off to the scene, to report back by radio on the equipment needed to salvage as much of the crashed aircraft as possible.

Too many interesting things happened at No. 3 B&GS for me to record them all here in detail. All the trades were well represented, and, as at Rockcliffe, we even had several GDs. Unlike Rockcliffe, the GDs at No. 3 B&GS were very usefully employed, and we often wondered why they didn't get trades pay. Their jobs were risky ones, and though at times they got on our nerves for one reason or another, we did respect them for the jobs they performed.

There was one sergeant GD in charge of a group of about twenty GDs. These were the men solely responsible for the entire drogue operation. They mended the drogues, they packed them, they calculated the scores on them, they winched the drogues from the bellies of the towing aircraft, and they cursed them. The system at Macdonald was similar to that at other units. The drogue was attached to a braided and twisted steel cable which could be winched out the belly of the aircraft. When an exercise was over, another drogue would be winched out, thus releasing the expended drogue, which fell to the ground close to a predetermined location. It was then picked up by a groundcrew GD to be marked, repaired if necessary, and repacked for future use. The scores were radioed back to the main station and the gunners advised.

Sometimes a drogue cable would foul up and seize on the winch. The aircraft could not land with a cable dragging, so it would have to be released one way or another, and accomplishing this could be extremely hazardous to the GD operator. On other occasions a drogue would unfurl too soon and begin to wind about the tail of the aircraft, and again it would be up to the GD operator to find a way to correct the problem. One operator had his hand badly mangled when trying to free a tangled drogue, and he suffered considerably before it was possible to get him back to the station and on to the hospital. These men were the real heroes of the station, but they never got the recognition they deserved. They received only basic flying pay and whatever rank they could scrounge from the OC of the drogue flight, who was their boss as well.

F/L Howard was another of the American gentlemen. He tried everything he could to get those boys a trade rating, but it was no go. They got the flying pay they so richly deserved, but that was all. There was one bright side to it for the GDs. They only had to fly a certain number of days in a month (I believe it was ten), to be able to draw a month's flying pay. Unless needed, the drogue operators flew only the minimum time required for their month's flying pay, and then worked on the range, picking up, scoring, and repairing, thus limiting the more dangerous work in the air to the shortest possible time.

F/L Howard recognized the need for good radio intercommunication on the drogue flights, something that was a real problem for the wireless section. Setting up the radio system was a snap—the difficulty lay with the GD drogue operators. They treated those headsets like so much garbage, tossing them aside at the end of a flight, leaving the wires tangled, dragging the wires on the ground, and so on. Then one day a pilot ordered an emergency bail-out. The GD drogue operator's headset wasn't working properly because the sleeve of the Plug 58 was severely scored from being trailed through the mud and so forth, and it was some time before the operator realized that the aircraft was in difficulty. That incident served as a better warning than all the haranguing that had gone before, and there were no more problems with the drogue operators on that score.

One of the Fairey Battles used as a drogue ship.

In July 1942 the problem of batteries for the ground station ATR5 became acute. Spares just were not available. I convinced the Supply Officer, S/L Avars, that there was no power supply in the RCAF Vocab that was designed or adequate for the job. (The Vocab was, and perhaps still is, a slang term for the Vocabulary, a catalogue of the parts and components available from RCAF supply depots.) He grudgingly signed a local purchase order (LPO) for about $75 so I

The Macdonald power supply.
On the top shelf is an R1082, and below it are two ATR5s.

No. 3 Bombing & Gunnery School   47

might buy the necessary parts to manufacture one. With the LPO in my pocket, I was off to Winnipeg to see what was available at the various radio parts wholesalers. Without too much difficulty I was able to find the chassis, tubes, sockets, transformers, chokes, and terminal strips needed, and I ordered the other parts, such as wire, power plugs, receptacles, and so forth, through the normal RCAF channels. (The order was expedited, which I hoped would ensure that we got the parts sometime that year!) Somehow, S/L Avars or one of his minions managed to get the expedite order to work, and in a week or so we had the ATR5 running on a power supply that worked off the normal 110 volts available from a wall receptacle. At least one battery in the transmitter/receiver was still necessary in the event of power failure, so that aircraft could be advised of the limitation to communications, but it was a far cry from the large number of batteries formerly needed to keep the unit operational. This type of successful experimentation was one of the things I most enjoyed about my work as a WOEM.

    Time had passed. I had arrived in Macdonald as an LAC, had soon been promoted to corporal, and then to sergeant. I had gained a fair understanding of the procedures involved in running an efficient wireless section, thanks to the excellent teachings of F/S Unit. Because of him, I was perhaps much more knowledgable than many of my peers. My previous military training had also been an asset, and I had the confidence that this instills. One day a posting came in for F/S Unit. We threw a going-away party for him at the famous Chan's Restaurant, next to the Wawaneesa Insurance Company's head office location on a side street in Portage. I was sorry to see him go, as we had become rather good friends, but it was the Air Force way, and he was overdue for the promotion to warrant officer that the posting involved. Shortly after he left Macdonald, I got the crown to add to my stripes, as I became a flight sergeant.
    I felt a great deal of satisfaction with this promotion. In the first place, as far as real rank was concerned, it was my first step up since the beginning of the war, as I had been a sergeant (confirmed) in the Army on mobilization day. In the second place, the promotion gave me a better wage. Finally, I was in charge of a section, which gave me the opportunity to determine for myself whether I had the leadership qualities needed for the next step—the one that every enlisted man yearns for—the elusive rank of warrant officer!

During the last years of my stay at Macdonald, my brother, who had enlisted into the RCAF as a photographer, was posted to No. 2 Air Transport Command Headquarters (ATCHQ) Winnipeg. It was pleasant to have some family near enough to visit. He had married about a year after I had, and while they were in Winnipeg his wife gave birth to a baby girl. My brother had never been satisfied with the accommodation situation, and after the happy addition to his family, his complaints became more vocal. Like most of the airmen, soldiers, and sailors posted away from their home cities, he and his family had been billetted with a family in the town where he was stationed. Most of us took it for granted that we would have to share quarters; there was no way we would be able to move furniture and effects about the country on our wages, even had it been possible to find the larger accommodation these would require. But my brother had grander ideas, and somehow or other his opinions got into the press. One of the Winnipeg newspapers ran an article about him and his small family and the privations they suffered. It was a real sob story, but, sad to say, I was completely unaware of it.

A few days after the article appeared, I was called into the Station Adjutant's office and advised that I had been posted to No. 2 ATCHQ on temporary duty for an unspecified period of time. I was to report immediately, so I packed a small bag, told Es what was up, and left for Winnipeg. As the Adjutant had directed, I reported to the AOC's secretary as soon as I arrived. The AOC (Air Officer Commanding) was *the* big cheese of the command, so I was astonished when the secretary immediately ushered me in to his office. He and an aide were waiting, and I quickly found out why I had been summoned. Didn't I know that an airman does NOT communicate with the press without ATCHQ approval? Didn't I know better than to let my brother open his big mouth? Didn't I realize that the article in the paper was not only in very bad taste, but was a black eye for the RCAF? The look on my face must have told them that I had no idea what they were talking about, for they stopped long enough to show me the paper. A quick skimming of the text and I realized what the AOC's harangue was all about, but I had to confess I didn't know why I had been called in. I could hardly be held responsible for my brother's actions, could I?

Oh, yes, I most certainly could! Though he was older, I was senior to my brother as far as the RCAF was concerned, and hence was more or less responsible for his utterings! I would have to clear up the problem, or I would find my brother stationed at Macdonald under my control (so to speak). If he had found the accommodation poor in Winnipeg, he would hate Macdonald! The AOC and his aide explained that if ATCHQ made an issue of the problem with an LAC, it would appear (and rightly so!) as if military pressure had been brought to bear, and the press would have a field day with it. On the other hand, if *I* spoke to him as a brother, the press would have no story. I had been given no choice, so I spoke with him, and the whole mess was quickly cleared up.

Our system of trades upgrading was called, appropriately enough, trade improvement, combining on-the-job training with formal lectures. These, supplemented by hands-on experience, should prepare a tradesman for the subsequent Trade Board examination and allow him to upgrade his trade grouping. The upgrading procedure presented few people with any problem, and the incentive of more money and a possible promotion ensured that the system was in active use at all times. Nonetheless, trade improvement was treated lightly by the RCAF, as the main objective for tradesmen on all BCATP stations was to keep the aircraft serviceable and flying so that aircrew could be trained and sent overseas, where they were so desperately needed.

Be all that as it may, in late '43 I received a signal from DAPS posting me to the School of Pedagogy at Rockcliffe, Ottawa. The course was to prepare me for the trade improvement lectures that were to be my responsibility on my return to Macdonald. On arrival in Ottawa I was advised that there was no accommodation on the station. I was to fend for myself, though I would, of course, be granted full subsistence allowance.

Fortunately, my previous posting to Rockcliffe had left me familiar with the Ottawa area, so I was able to find suitable lodgings without difficulty. Returning to the station to become acquainted with the others on my course, I was surprised to learn that I was the only wireless type on the course. There were no two NCOs on the course that were in the same trade. In the Sergeants' Mess later that day I ran into a certain GD sergeant, and I spent a few minutes reminding him of the extreme injustice he had done me and some of my associates a few years back. The fact that I was now a flight sergeant while he was still a sergeant did a great deal, I am sure, to persuade him to hold his tongue and not sound off, as he had done to us those few years earlier. Poor Sgt. Stese! He and I were to meet again in 1965, in Clinton, at which time I would be a warrant officer while he would still be a sergeant.

Ah yes, the School of Pedagogy—that was a real tongue-twister. I'm still convinced that name was chosen for no other reason than its impressive sound. The School of Instructional Technique, which it was renamed many years later, made much more sense. Name aside, the course was all that it was cracked up to be—intensive, professional, and effective. The instructors were all civilian educators who knew their business; I believe that the only members of the school who were not civilian were the clerical staff, the School Warrant Officer, and the OC. At any rate, it was a delight to attend class. Everything was fascinating and well taught, so you just couldn't fail to learn what the instructors were attempting to put across.

I can still remember some of the sample lessons, proof that the course was effective. One was by a W&B refrigeration technician, who used a few simple home-brew training aids to demonstrate how the defrost cycle of a refrigerator works. Another lesson was by a clerk, who stepped out of his trade to give an interesting lesson on the use of a sliding sinker and three-way swivel in still fishing!

All good things must come to an end, as the old saw goes, and a few weeks later I completed the course. I felt full of grits and vinegar, ready to take on the world and to advance the trade improvement classes to the full. It was on to Macdonald and No. 3 B&GS!

Of course, back at No. 3 B&GS, on-the-job training was still the most popular method of trade improvement, despite my eagerness to use the techniques I had learned at the School of Pedagogy. There were some formal classes and lectures, but these were often put aside due to the pressure of work. The aircraft had to be kept serviceable for training the aircrew, and if that meant that trades lectures were postponed or cancelled, so be it. A lot of our time was spent transferring radios from one aircraft to another; with more BCATP stations open, radios were in short supply and had to be shared between aircraft. There were never enough radios to equip the serviceable aircraft those days.

With my instructional skills barely tested, I was given another posting, this time to No. 5 Radio School, Clinton, Ontario, where I would attend a conversion course. The brass in Ottawa had decided that being a wireless mechanic was not enough; every senior wireless mechanic was to take his turn at the Clinton conversion course to learn all about radar. There was no warning given; it was just a case of GO! . . . NOW!

It quickly became apparent to those of us on the conversion course that No. 5 Radio School was run by the same rules as a concentration camp. The domestic area of the station was normal, but the school was surrounded by an electrified, barbed-wire fence. Guard towers loomed over every gate, and the gates themselves were manned around the clock by AFPs (Air Force Police, sometimes known as Service police). Admission to the compound was by pass only. Any book was allowed in, but not even a notebook was allowed back out without going through a complicated safety procedure; any book to be taken out had to be submitted to the school monitor's office, where it was vetted and then sent on to the guard house, where it could be picked up by the owner upon showing his pass. This discouraged outside study, which was probably the idea. (We were told that the electronic technique was so different from what was the norm to us wireless types, that we would only confuse ourselves by studying without some direction from an instructor. What trust our superiors had!)

That course I attended at Clinton in 1944 was the first real technical course in electronics that I had in the RCAF. Previous ones in high school and the Army had been quite elementary, and I had absolutely no idea what I was in for, what methods would be used, or what state of preparation would be demanded of me. I was ready to participate to the best of my ability, but I knew I would encounter considerable problems. It would be difficult for anyone to understand my position unless they had "walked in my moccasins", so suffice it to say that I was anticipating a rough time. As it turned out, my expectations were not disappointed.

There were a variety of wireless types on the course, which was designated WMR(1), meaning Wireless Mechanic to Radar, Conversion Course No. 1. My troubles started on Day One. There was next to no introduction to the course, and the instructors were all radar types who appeared (note that I say "appeared" only) to resent the fact that we wireless mechanics were being told the secrets of their trade. They were obviously not graduates of the School of Pedagogy, with its methods for effective teaching. Some of these men could probably have made excellent WMs, but most were radar types, through and through. They knew their own trade, but were more lost in ours than we were in theirs, and they certainly weren't teachers. Nor did they take into consideration the fact that we hadn't asked for this course; it was the idea of the brass in Ottawa.

At any rate, we were definitely considered outsiders. Radar was still a new marvel, and because of its classified nature, some of those trained in the technique had a sense of extreme superiority. Even in the mess we seemed to be bundled aside as so much trash. Our course represented the only wireless men at the school. It certainly wasn't a comfortable feeling, and no one on staff made any overtures to change the situation. Initially, I knew no one on the course, as most were Permanent Force types I had never had occasion to run into. Our nearly unanimous bewilderment, confusion, and sense of isolation from the rest of the school served to form friendships among us quickly.

As it was to be a six-month course, I had gone to considerable expense to bring Es with me to Clinton. The trip from Macdonald, Manitoba to Clinton, Ontario had drained our savings, but I could see no sense in leaving Es alone in Portage la Prairie for that length of time. We had no problem finding accommodation for Es in Clinton. By this time we had acclimatized ourselves to living in other people's houses, subjecting ourselves to their rules, using their facilities, and so forth. Clinton was a nice little town, and we enjoyed living there once we got over the feeling that we were being scanned by everyone we passed. As there were few airmen and their wives living there, everyone knew your name, rank, and function at the station almost as soon as you arrived in Clinton.

If the living conditions were comfortable and the town pleasant to live in, the course itself was a real worry. The pure theory was more than I could handle cold, though I felt sure that had I been given a month or so to prepare for the course, I could have managed. I couldn't seem to get the hang of what the instructors were trying to put across, and they made absolutely no effort to soften the blow or to change the method of attack. I burned a lot of midnight oil, both in the compound and at home, but after a few months I admitted defeat. At a requested interview with the Chief Instructor (CI), I suggested that I voluntarily cease training. The CI, W/C Rogers, agreed to the suggestion, but added the proviso, which I was to appreciate later, that I would be able to return to the school at my own request when I decided the time was right.

Es and I regretfully packed our effects and headed back to Macdonald, poorer but wiser. The trip back was completely uneventful, and again, finding accommodation in Portage la Prairie was no problem, as we knew who to ask and what to look for. Actually, our lodgings were perhaps the best we had ever had in Portage.

Knowing I would eventually have to take the radar course, and determined to do it well, I contacted the station education officer as soon as I was back at Macdonald. With his assistance, I obtained the necessary books and so forth to prepare me for that day. He also told me later that the average grade in the class I had left was not very high, so I had hopes that the school brass would do something about the teaching methods before I returned for my second attempt.

RCAF stations always had something going on in the way of recreation, even during the war. At No. 3 B&GS we were blessed with an RC chaplain who loved GOOD MUSIC (the capital letters are his). He enjoyed opera and the classics, and once he learned that Es loved to play concert music, he visited us at every opportunity. He even enjoyed the scales and exercises, though I must admit that I sometimes tired of them, and he made every effort possible to help Es in her studies. He managed to get time for her whenever she needed it at the theatre or chapel, both of which had a decent piano. In turn, she would play his favourites whenever she could.

The chaplain had a rather extensive record library, which travelled about with him as he was posted to various stations across the country. The records were all 78s, of course, and were all quite thick, heavy, and fragile. Even our moving bill seemed steep and we travelled light, so I can imagine how the chaplain's must have been.

Show companies, somewhat like the American USO shows, often toured the camps and stations to entertain the troops. These groups usually recruited someone from the station they were visiting, to personalize the show and get a bigger laugh out of the boys. In one case, our photographic section (all two of them) was invited to participate in an Egyptian dance. The two servicemen were a typical Mutt and Jeff pair; the senior was a trifle chubby, and the junior was slight but had a very hairy chest. The costuming was kept simple; sundae cup inserts were taped to their chests as brassieres, and new mops were chopped up to provide wigs. The biggest laughs came when the cups, poorly attached as they were, began to come off due to the vigor of the men's gyrations.

Some of the wives worked as volunteer hostesses at the local servicemen's canteens. One day a problem arose when a black serviceman from the nearby Southport Air Observer's School walked in. No one could understand a word he said, nor could they agree what foreign language he was speaking. Slowing his speech to a turtle's pace, he eventually made them understand he was actually speaking English. A Jamaican, he had been educated in Scotland, and the resulting burr was something one could cut with a knife! When speaking at his usual quick pace, he was completely incomprehensible. With this incident as an introduction, he quickly became a friend and favoured customer.

Another occasion that comes to mind took place one New Year's Eve. With a group of other married couples, Es and I were invited to make the rounds that evening. My wife happened to be the only dark-haired woman in the group, and at one residence the lady of the house insisted that Es be the first one in the door. She didn't consider herself superstitious; it was just a matter of taking no chances. (The first person in the door after the break of the New Year determines the year's fortune—if dark-haired, good luck will dominate; if light-haired, bad luck.) Moose milk was the drink that year at Portage. Similar to egg nog, it was at least doubly as potent, but it looked and tasted so innocent, only the very determined could nurse just one small cup at each residence. Somehow or other, Es and I managed to stay sober that particular New Year's Eve, though there were a great many who didn't.

A number of the people who let rooms to servicemen or their wives didn't want the bother of children in their homes. I couldn't comprehend such an attitude then, though today I can understand. In Portage, seven or eight of the servicemen's wives met daily at one of the local coffee-bars, I believe it was the Mayfair Hotel. One of these young women was pregnant, and her landlady told her that after her baby was born, there would no longer be a room for her at that house. No Human Rights Code nor tenant's protection group was around in those days; all one could depend on was common decency, and apparently the same ideas were not shared by all. The desire of the other women in the coffee group to see that justice did prevail was the only help available for the young mother-to-be. Her husband was a trainee on one of the courses at No. 3 B&GS, and she didn't wish to bother him about this problem unless she had no choice, for he was worrying enough about passing the exams on his course. Even the other wives were only told in desperation when she could find no solution on her own.

In the course of time the young wife was finally admitted to hospital. Just before the baby was born, the other wives, *en masse*, went to visit the landlady in question. Would she reconsider? She refused; her rooms could be rented or denied to whomever she pleased. Expecting this attitude, the women proceeded with Plan B. They reminded the landlady that they met all the incoming trains and buses which brought the wives of new trainees or staff members. It would be a simple matter to see that none of the new arrivals ever learned of the rooms to let at this particular house. In effect, the landlady could and would be blackballed. Yes, diapers could indeed be a serious problem—water was so expensive and the house had no laundering facilities—but the other wives would share in the cleaning, so there wouldn't be a problem, would there? Then there was the noise the baby would make. But that was a very natural thing, wasn't it, and couldn't the complaint wait upon the fact? The landlady finally agreed to let the young mother stay. She went to visit her at the hospital and assured her that she and her baby would be welcomed at her home. She would even look in the attic to see if she still had her daughter's bassinet and a few other trifles to make everything as comfortable as possible for their return. Now, it's true there was no such thing at that time as women's power, but who needed it when there was a group of seven or eight friends to take whatever steps were necessary in the cause of justice.

There were two movie houses in Portage la Prairie and one at the B&GS. We usually only attended the one at the B&GS on Sundays, for on that day the other two were closed. There was an unwritten rule that the first Sunday showing was attended by the single men at the station, and the second was more or less allotted to the married men and their wives. It was the only day there were two screenings, and it was normally the first night of any new shows. Seating capacity was limited, so everyone tended to take their turn.

The two theatres in Portage were regular commercial enterprises. One was an independent theatre operated by a Mr. Mell and his wife. They lived in a special apartment they had had built between the theatre and the building adjacent to it. The apartment was only ten or twelve feet wide and two stories high, but it was very comfortable. Es and I came to know Mr. and Mrs. Mell well, and occasionally went on picnics with their family.

The other theatre was one of the Playhouse syndicate. It was very efficiently managed by a Mr. Torp. One evening Es and I were at the Playhouse, pleasantly anticipating a first-class, first-run movie. At the appointed time the lights dimmed, the movie started . . . but there was no sound! After a few moments the lights went up again, and Mr. Torp mounted the stage to annouce that there was a problem with the projectors. If the audience would file out, everyone would be refunded their money. The theatre would be closed until the Playhouse chain's maintenance people could get to Portage to effect the necessary repairs. With a lot of the audience sitting for a moment to chat and discuss the excitement, there was no mass exodus. As Mr. Torp went past my seat, I stopped him to suggest that I might be able to do something to get the projectors operating on at least a jury-rig basis. Mr. Torp was a quick to grasp at any opportunity, and he grasped at this one.

Upstairs in the projection room I gasped at the scene. The theatre was using some of the most antiquated and out-moded equipment it had ever been my misfortune to see. Also, the projectionist was just that and no more; he certainly wasn't a good housekeeper. A thick layer of dust lay on everything that didn't need to move.

The dust was part of the problem, which was quickly rectified. There appeared to be no cooling system or air circulation about a bit of sleeving that fed the wires from the sound cell to the amplifiers. As there was considerable heat in that area, the sleeving had melted, losing its insulation factor, and this effectively stopped the sound. After blowing away most of the dust that surrounded the air vents, I asked the projectionist to get me a straw from the soda bar downstairs. I used the straw as insulated sleeving to replace that which had melted, and turned on the machine to find that it worked. I used the same procedure on the other machine, then left the projectionist to his job and went downstairs to tell Mr. Torp he could stop being a soda jerk and become a theatre manager once more. A few minutes later the movie was started again, and we all thoroughly enjoyed it.

During the show, Mr. Torp sat down beside me and suggested that we have a cup of coffee together in his office after the show. We had done this before, so thought nothing of it as we accepted his invitation. Imagine our surprise when we arrived in his office to find a beautiful bouquet of flowers for Es and a little card in an envelope for me. That card can still be found in one of my scrapbooks, and it reads something like this:

>TO WHOM IT MAY CONCERN
>(YOU KNOW WHO)
>ADMIT BEARER
>(and guest)
>April 21/44—April 1st/45
>(Signed, Mr. Torp)

We were real movie buffs, so that generous gift came in very handy. There wasn't a show that we didn't see, but I did try hard not to abuse that little card.

 Somehow I was volunteered (as is normally the case in the Air Force) for duties with the new air cadet squadron. It was to be sponsored by the local Lion's Club and St. Mary's Parish. I later learned that Mr. Torp was a head lion or some such thing, and was also quite prominent in the parish. Perhaps that accounted for the volunteering! The command liaison officer was Flying Officer J. Diefenbaker, a name which meant nothing to me at the time, who mentioned to me one time that his brother had some influence in Ottawa if we ever needed it.

 I learned more from those kids than they were aware they knew. They were very co-operative, and we enjoyed our association to the fullest. The biggest kick they got out of air cadets was the silent drill we invented for them. First we had them go through a series of manoeuvres on the drill square while we shouted out the traditional commands. The drill was repeated and repeated until the commands were merely grunts marking the time each new movement was to begin. Then even the grunts were left out, and all that was necessary was to start the cadets. The exercise was a complete success and one that they enjoyed tremendously, as did the inspecting team from Command. Whether or not this procedure was then used at any other cadet squadrons, we were not aware, but to us it was an achievement.

One thing I somehow managed to avoid was to pull a night shift. On those rare occasions when I did work at night, everyone else did, too. For example, we might be having night exercises, so the whole station would be alerted and we all worked though the night.

I recall one particular such night, when the moon was bright and the sky was clear. Exercises had been put on, and I was elected to go up in one of the Ansons to check out a peculiar radio problem. The radio operated correctly on the ground, but as soon as the Anson was airborne, the radio packed up completely. The Anson was a Mark V, one of the plywood jobs, and had been declared serviceable and unserviceable so many times, the L14 was full, a situation I found less than reassuring.

As we prepared for takeoff and taxied down the runway, the radio kept us in contact with the control tower, but we were no sooner airborne than it shut down. But what the pilot and the rest of the crew had neglected to report was that all the facilities on the radio operator's table went out, not just the radio. It was not a radio problem, but an electrical malfunction. While the pilot concentrated on the night exercise, I did a little detective work. It was quickly apparent that the fuse that fed power to the radio table was intact, but when the aircraft became airborne an ever-so-slight shift of weight caused the fuse holder to open up at that point. As a result, contact between the service and the fuse was lost. A slight bend with a pair of needle-nose pliers, and the radio table came back to life.

Now that the radio was willing to work properly, I began to feel the effects of being airborne myself, and shifted position to be more at ease. I had found that the only place I could feel comfortable in an Anson was seated on or near the main spar. This was the point of balance, and I felt less subject to airsickness there than when I sat elsewhere. It was funny, but while I was working, I had absolutely no ill sensations; the moment I was not occupied with some chore, a slight feeling of nausea hit me. Self-induced? Possibly.

The exercise completed, we were within sight of the runway lights when the pilot aborted the landing. The landing gear had gone down, but the "locked" indicator had not come on. Now, this Anson, as I mentioned, was made of plywood; there was no strong steel belly, like the Goblin had, to support the craft in emergency landings. Furthermore, there were about 20 aircraft in the circuit, all running low on fuel, and they had to be brought in safely before the tower could concentrate on us. We were put on hold, and the pilot climbed to the ordered altitude to make a series of large circuits. I was starting to feel just a little bit queasy, through I was promised by our chubby, cigar-smoking, Yankee contract pilot that he would make it down okay. It was just a matter of getting the other aircraft out of the way first, in the event that the landing gear was indeed not fully down and locked. We couldn't afford to block a runway with all those other fellows still wanting to come in, could we? Somehow, that didn't reassure me as much as the pilot seemed to expect.

We finally got the word to come in for a few passes, so the chaps on the ground could see whether our gear appeared to be all the way down or not and determine whether we should land on the grass or on the runway. After the first pass, our pilot was told to fly over again, but a trifle lower. That pass was low, but rather too long, so our pilot became confused as he resumed altitude, made a navigational error, and ended up about 12 miles south of the field. Neither he nor any of the rest of us in the aircraft realized this, as our radio contact was still loud and clear. The station suggested that as the runways were clear, our pilot was to try to come in slowly and touch down as lightly as possible. He did a good job, touching down ever so gently on the runway. The moment the wheels met the landing surface, the "locked" indicator came on. We went off the end of the runway by about ten feet and bogged down in the mud, but we were all too relieved to be down safely to be much concerned.

Within moments a vehicle was there to pick us up, but I realized immediately that something was not quite right. The vehicle's markings were certainly not those of our base, and the unfamiliar driver was obviously a civilian. We were at an Air Force station all right, but it wasn't No. 3 B&GS, but No. 5 AOS, Southport! We were driven to the Officers' Mess, where the CO of the AOS welcomed us. He had already been in contact with our CO, who had asked that we be transported back to Macdonald without delay, as he had a few words for the pilot of our aircraft. We were silent as we climbed into the truck and began to head back to Macdonald, but after a few minutes, we let our poor pilot have it. I don't know if you remember the story of Wrong Way Corrigan, but that's the title this particular pilot had to live with for the rest of his RCAF career! We later discovered that the setting of the microswitch controlling the power to the "locked" indicator was out of adjustment. It took little time to re-adjust the setting and to check all the Ansons for a similar problem. Our CO wanted no recurrences!

60 *The War Years*

One cool winter's day we had some reason to celebrate; it may have been a recent major victory in the war overseas. At any rate, a number of makeshift floats were hurriedly prepared for parading around the station. The one from Works and Buildings was unique; being towed along in a bathtub was Sandy the plumber, apparently in the altogether and well supplied with liquid refreshment, sporting a Hitler moustache and a German field helmet. He saluted all and sundry in the well known Heil Hitler fashion, quite immune to the cold weather. I imagine he got Heil from his good woman later, but at the time, he was certainly enjoying himself!

Sgt Sandy gives "Heil" to Hitler!

Summers at Macdonald could be pleasant, but winters were another thing entirely. Even an ex-Montrealer like myself found them blood-freezing. The winter of 1942 was one of the coldest. On one March morning the snow started just after we arrived at the station. Flying was cancelled for the day, giving us the opportunity to do some of those repairs that weren't vital, but would increase the efficiency of the equipment. We spent all morning tinkering with a tuning here, a minor adjustment there, then waded through the snow to the mess for lunch. There were a few more drifts to climb over as we returned to the hangar to spend the afternoon on a general clean-up and a few more repairs. We had work to do, and paid the weather little mind. Our shop had been moved from the runway side of the hangar to the other side, so we didn't even pay much heed to the station's four snowblowers being on the runways all day, in echelon formation, clearing away the snow. They only stopped for fuel and to change drivers. When we were ready to leave for home, we discovered that snow had completely covered the door leading outside, but fortunately our shop had another door leading into the hangar, from where we were able to get out. When we arrived back the next morning, we were amazed at the volume of snow that had fallen over that 24-hour period. One of the hangars had snow right up to the roof-top, until the Works and Buildings boys cleared it away. Sometime during the night, the W&B boys had also cleared the roof of our shop lean-to, as they were afraid the roof might collapse under the weight of the snow.

Es and I were living at the house of an elderly lady, Mrs. Sound, who also let rooms to the station Adjutant's wife and to one of the pilots from our station. We were the youngest couple, and in their eyes, I guess we were the most expendable. In any case, the house had been completely snowed in, and Mrs. Sound had been caught with her cupboards bare! (At least, there was no milk nor fresh bread in the house.) Snow had fallen and drifted up to the tops of the front door, rear door, and all the lower floor windows. The other occupants of the house coaxed, pleaded, and finally prevailed upon Es, as the youngest, to slide down from the second story window, taking a sled with her, and go for provisions. They promised to either have a rope ready to pull her up when she returned, or to have sufficient snow cleared from one of the doors to allow her back in. I'm not certain how they did it, but one of the doors was shovelled out by the time Es returned, though I believe it was done by a kind neighbour who saw Es sliding down that impromptu toboggan run and took pity on her. All's well that ends well, but to this day, Es keeps enough provisions in our home for a week ahead!

The toboggan run.

No. 3 Bombing and Gunnery School

We had our comedies, of course. The ATR5 we used as a ground station for the control tower was remote-controlled, and a speaker in our shop kept us informed of everything said by the operator at the tower. At times, the continual tower chatter blaring into the shop was a distracting nuisance, so we devised a method of cutting off the air signal with a switch whenever it wasn't necessary for us to hear what was going on. The current tower operator's nickname was Pud, so one of the wags in the section labelled the switch "Pud in" and "Pud out". (A wag, that is, a wiseacre or joker, was something entirely different from a WAG, or Wireless Air Gunner. The latter would not have appreciated any comparison!)

Rumble funds were very, very illegal. But if someone, through carelessness or stupitidy, caused someone else extra work, then the common consensus was that he deserved some simple punishment, or better yet, a voluntary fine. This fine was termed a rumble, and put into a rumble fund. (The name probably came from the fact that there was a rumble going about that someone had done something stupid!) For example, if someone carelessly pulled the D-ring of a parachute, the safety equipment section would have to go through the entire exercise of checking and repacking that chute for no reason beyond someone else's stupidity. The perpetrator would be fined by the safety section, and the money would go into the safety section's rumble fund. Various sections had these illegal funds, and they usually provided for an annual or semi-annual party.

The wireless section's rumble fund was kept supplied by any airman or drogue operator who climbed out of his aircraft without removing the plug of his headset from the socket mounted in the aircraft. The headset cords, the plugs they terminated in, and the sockets mounted in the aircraft were in direly short supply. Even though the equipment provided a crucial lifeline for the aircrew, it was next to impossible to impress this upon them until the moment of truth arrived. In any case, if the headset was carted out of the aircraft without the plug having been removed, one of two things happened: the plug was pulled clear and the wires in the cord were broken; or the socket was torn from its mounting and the aircraft had to be taken out of service while the socket was replaced. The socket was only mounted to the aircraft frame with a heavy section of Barbour's twine, so that in an emergency the twine would break. We certainly didn't mind if someone pulled out the socket or damaged the wires in an emergency, but under normal conditions, such damage was only caused by stupidity. On the many occasions when this happened, our section's rumble fund was increased. Our fund was hidden under a "man in a barrel" which sat on my desk. When the barrel was lifted, exposing the naked man, a small drawer in the base opened, and this was where our money was kept.

One morning, as was his practice, our CO, G/C Garb, was first on the line to get a drogue ship out. Over our speaker ("Pud in") we heard the tower give him clearance, but there was no reply from the

The morning line-up at Macdonald, Manitoba.

drogue ship. A second clearance was given, again with no reply. A few moments later we heard an aircraft revving its engine a few yards from our shop door, a signal that the aircraft had radio trouble. One of the men grabbed a headset and went out to clear up the problem. In seconds we heard him calling up the tower—the problem, we thought, must have been a minor one. Our man came back into the shop, declaring that he had found nothing wrong, and we went back to work.

The next thing we heard was the tower once again giving the aircraft clearance for takeoff. No reply. By this time, eight or nine drogue ships had become airborne, and the CO had lost his favourite spot as first aircraft out. Again we heard the aircraft revving its engine outside our door. (Was it our imagination, or did the engine rev just a little longer and just a little louder?) At any rate, one of the corporals ran out with a headset this time, and, again, we heard him contact the tower a few seconds later.

As soon as the aircraft was back in position, the tower gave clearance. Silence from the aircraft. As we watched from the door, we saw the CO's aircraft begin taxiing toward us, but he ignored the taxi strip and came roaring across the grass, something he never would have done in normal circumstances. I quickly asked the AC and corporal how they had checked the aircraft and what they had done. Each of them gave me the same answer: they had gone under the belly, stuck their heads up into the drogue pit, plugged in, and contacted the tower. It was up to me to deal with our fuming CO, so I grabbed a headset and was waiting for the aircraft when it came up to the hangar doors. Climbing up onto the port side, where the pilot's Socket 29 was, I motioned for the CO to open his cowling. Scarlet-faced with anger, he slammed open the cowling with a bang, but said nothing. A glance into the cockpit told me the story, and I slid down, scrambled under the aircraft to the starboard side, where I could not be seen from the tower, and wiggled the aileron to get the CO's attention. I then pulled my headset's Plug 58 from my pocket and with great exaggeration pantomimed plugging it into a socket. The old man looked blank for a moment, then slammed shut the cowling. He hadn't plugged in his headset! As I ran back to the shelter of the hangar door, he revved up and taxied away.

This time when the tower gave him clearance, we could hear the CO reply with a radio check before he took off. The wireless section knew what had happened, as they had all been watching, but they were smart enough to say nothing about it to anyone else, then or later. We had all put the incident from our minds when the shop door banged open a couple of hours later. There stood the old man. "I know you have a rumble fund here somewhere, and I owe! Where is it?" One of the men pointed to the man-in-a-barrel on my desk. Lifting the barrel, the CO dropped a five-dollar bill into the drawer; that was a lot of money in those days. "A bloody fool like me should pay double, shouldn't he?" he grumbled, and he was gone. That's the kind of CO anyone could relate to.

Insofar as uniforms were concerned, trouser leg widths were the only real bone of contention. Issue trousers came with stovepipe legs, somewhat like modern blue jeans. This was not only a trifle uncomfortable, but it made for some difficulty in keeping the trousers pressed. Further, I had always been in the habit of putting my boots or shoes on first, and then pulling on my trousers, which was quite impossible with the issue trousers. The popular solution was to have a tailor insert a wedge of the same or similar material into the inside seam of the pant leg. With a careful pressing, the pants would look quite acceptable . . . for a while. Unfortunately, the materials rarely came from the same batch, so after a few cleanings, the colour match was off. The alteration, which was quite illegal, became obvious, and this sometimes resulted in disciplinary action for the wearer.

The perfect solution came from a tailor (the only one) in Portage. His son was an enlisted airman, so he sympathized with me when I told him of my problem. He came up with a simple but effective answer. "The next time you get a pair of uniform trousers," he advised me, "ask for a pair two or three sizes larger than you normally take. They'll be much too large for you, but pay that no mind, because the leg width will be what you want. Bring them to me, and I'll take your measurements and tailor the trousers to fit." With my next pair of trousers I did just that, and I continued to follow his suggestion with every pair of uniform trousers from then until after the war, when they were again styled so that they could be slid on over your boots.

Speaking of boots, I had a small problem with those, as well. Army boots had never bothered me, but the Air Force boots rubbed uncomfortably against my ankle bone. It was not a serious dilemma; boots were only required on parade, and I could wear shoes at other times. I could have asked the MO (Medical Officer) for permission to wear shoes on parade, but I didn't feel that that was really the thing to do. I tried everything I could think of to alleviate the discomfort, even hammering at the boot-tops in an effort to soften them, but all was to no avail. Taking a cue from my experience with the tailor, I took the boots to the town shoemaker, hoping he would know a way to make the tops putty-soft. After listening to my tale, the shoemaker told me to leave the boots with him and he would have an answer within a day or two. When I returned to the shop a few days later, I found that the shoemaker had cut off the boot-tops and sewn a finishing seam along the remaining cut edge. To the inspecting eye on the parade square it would appear that I was wearing regulation boots, but my feet would know they were wearing comfortable shoes. The shoemaker had reasoned that the boot-tops were invisible beneath the pant-leg anyway. These civvies knew their business.

We had two COs while I was at No. 3 B&GS. The first, Group Captain Man, was of the old school, a typical Permanent Force officer. He demanded discipline and absolute obedience, but as he set a good example, asking nothing of his men that he didn't ask of himself, he received the full respect and co-operation of everyone on the station. One incident proved to me that his method was without doubt effective. I had recently been promoted to sergeant, and on this particular day I was the orderly sergeant, paired with a very junior officer who had never been orderly officer before. Though my senior in rank, he was depending on me to lead him through the day, and I was relying on my previous experience in the Army to see *me* through the day, as the Station Orders for that day were a trifle skimpy, to say the least. At about 11:45 we headed off to the Airmen's Mess to check on the noon meal. The normal procedure in the Army had been to enter the mess hall, call the room to attention, ask for complaints, and leave. Our CO had a different idea. The orders stated that the orderly officer, accompanied by the orderly sergeant, must eat at least one meal in the Airmen's Mess. This was normally to be the noon meal. We were about 100 yards from the building when we heard a burst of angry voices from the mess,. As the uproar continued, the young officer began quaking in his boots.

"What do we do?" he asked.

I suggested that we go in to determine the problem. He demurred, and wondered if we shouldn't get a police escort. I countered by saying that as he represented the CO, this situation might be something the CO could best handle himself. With little hesitation he was off to the CO's office. I stayed where I was, reflecting that if I had been in his boots, I would much rather have entered the mess than called in the CO to do my job for me!

About ten minutes went by, and I was surprised to see the CO returning with the orderly officer. I guess the CO felt sympathy for the young sprog officer. The three of us entered the mess by the kitchen door. The CO quickly sized up the situation simply by asking the mess sergeant what was on the menu. He then entered the mess proper, and no sooner was he through that door than the uproar ceased. He removed his hat, put it under his arm, and stepped to the head of the line at the food service table, motioning for the orderly officer and myself to follow him. We each picked up a plate, and the servers dished out the meal of corn on the cob, baked potatoes, pork chops, and I believe either peas or carrots. Only a few other staff members had begun eating by that time. None of the trainees had even picked up a plate to be served, though there were at least a hundred of them. With the orderly officer and I taking our cue from the old man, the three of us sat down and began to eat. The CO's quiet example impressed me so much, that to this day I can picture him buttering his corn, salting it, and beginning to eat. Within seconds the trainees were shuffling into line and being served. It was only afterward that the CO explained the problem to us. Apparently the trainees who had created all the fuss were RNZAF, RAAF, and RAF. To them, corn was pig food, and they were damned if they would be forced to eat pig food for their lunch! But when a group captain, together with his orderly officer and orderly sergeant, sat down and ate corn on the cob, they realized it must be good enough for them, too. There was no more complaining, nor was there any subsequent lecturing—nothing. We stayed a little longer than usual, and when the CO went up for a second helping of corn, it broke the ice completely and some of the trainees went up for seconds, too! The CO had handled a potentially explosive situation in the simplest and most effective way possible, and at the same time strengthened the respect we all felt for him.

Our second CO was W/C Garb, who was promoted to G/C soon after arriving at Macdonald. Where G/C Man was an experienced officer, long accustomed to his exalted rank, W/C Garb had been a Permanent Force armourer in peacetime. He had managed to get on a pilot's course and graduated as a sergeant pilot. On declaration of war, or shortly before, he had been commissioned, and since then had worked his way up quickly till he was now CO of No. 3 B&GS. He flew one of the drogue aircraft, and it was soon apparent that he could do anything that anyone else in his trade could, and perhaps a trifle better. Quite a bit younger than our previous CO, he seemed to fit into the picture better.

At that time we were experiencing an extreme shortage of Sockets 29. G/C Garb came to the shop to discuss the problem with us. Was there nothing else that would do? Could we not devise a substitute? Could we not wire in headsets so that the same one could be used by various aircrew, and thus reduce the wear and tear? and so on. Well, there were no easy answers, and insofar as safety was concerned, there was no substitute. The only solution was for the aircrew to take better care. Accepting our expertise, G/C Garb then issued an instruction, which was duly published in the Daily Routine Orders, to the effect that as damage to the plugs and sockets had reached epidemic proportions, future damage through neglect would result in disciplinary action. The work involved in changing these items and the unavailability of replacements was creating a situation in which flying might have to be curtailed, and he, the CO, would deal with any offenders personally.

For a short spell there was a natural reduction in damage, but one day we were called in to inspect a turret in a Bolingbroke. A Socket 29, pulled completely off its mountings, was wedged in between the turret and the frame. The plug was still inserted in the socket, and the cord attached to the plug had been torn from the headset. Some student, of course, had the balance of the headset. We removed the damaged components, replaced the socket, and signed the aircraft serviceable once more. The problem of disciplinary action we left to the OC of the flight concerned.

Bristol Bolingbrokes in formation.

A day or so later I was called in as a witness at the trial of the RAAF trainee who had caused the damage. He was charged with neglect, and, as was typical of our RAAF and RNZAF students, he pleaded "Not Guilty". I was a trifle surprised by the CO's mild manner, as the offence was a direct contravention of his own order, duly published, but . . . who was I to say? The CO placed an E26, for $5, I believe, in front of the man and suggested that he sign it, and the matter would be forgotten. The $5, he said, would pay for the neglect and damage, and no crime would appear on the trainee's documents. "No, Sir," was the response. He would be damned if he would pay for anything. The CO's manner heated up considerably. If the trainee wouldn't sign the E26, the CO would sign it for him and award the trainee a few days in jail as well, to remind him of his position. There was no response, so the trainee spent two or three days languishing in jail. After that, the damage situation decreased dramatically. I don't think G/C Man could have handled it any better, but I often wonder what he would have done.

During the early part of the war, we had to tolerate general inspections by a high authority similar to the Army's Inspector General. (I cannot recall the title of this particular position, but I am certain it was senior to the Air Officer Commanding of a Command.) Everything had to be spic and span clean for these inspections to impress these senior officers, though what real good this did was beyond me—it would have been better for them to see the station as it really was in working order. Even the dress we had to wear during these inspections was such that if a job had to be done, the uniforms would be ruined. Just imagine an aero-engine mechanic in his best uniform working on an engine!

One spring day we were notified that the station was to be inspected and everything was to be made immaculate. I had just lost about half my crew to overseas transfers, and the replacements were not due for at least a week. (When a man was transferred overseas, he naturally took the balance of the leave he was entitled to for that year, added whatever embarkation leave he had coming, plus any travelling time, and took off to enjoy his last few days or weeks in Canada with his family and friends.) Though my section was sadly lacking in manpower, there was no reduction in work, as the station had no respect for the fact that we were short-handed. It was my view that the most important function of the wireless section was to keep the aircraft's radios fully operational. We had other responsibilities as well, such as keeping 150 or so headsets in A1 condition and maintaining the serviceability of all other electronic devices on the station—intercoms, the ground station, the morse instruction equipment, and so forth. To make the place as spotless as it normally was for inspections we would have had to delay our work, and this was contrary to my instincts and training. When I described my problem to the Station Adjutant, who in the absence of a signals officer acted as my mentor, he merely stated the obvious: "Do what you can".

We did the most important thing first—ensured that all equipment was in serviceable condition. Next was the clean-up, which we did to the best of our ability in the time frame allotted. The least important item, dress, was left to the end. I made certain that the men all had their best uniforms in their lockers, ready to wear, but that was as far as I would permit them to go. There was work still to be done, and only if there was time after the inspecting party arrived on the station would they be allowed to put on their best blues at the last moment. We had one corporal who acted as a job dispatcher, in effect a desk job, and he was permitted to wear his good uniform. The others wore their everyday battle dress, which was certainly not the order of the day. I did make certain that these uniforms were as clean and well pressed as possible.

The brass arrived on the station without any warning of the exact time. After the usual preliminaries they headed to the drogue hangar for inspection. We were directly in the line of their approach, so we were the first hangar staff that the Inspector General saw. The first we knew of their arrival was when the SWO opened the door to our shop and called my men to attention. I came down from my office to greet the inspecting party, and was met by a glare from the SWO and a look of surprise from the CO—they had obviously seen what uniforms my men were wearing. The inspector didn't appear to notice, although I am quite sure he did. He asked the usual questions, including one about my staff and the establishment. (The establishment was the suggested quota of personnel, by rank and trade, for a section.) Speaking the truth, despite the continuing glare of the SWO, I replied that on paper, I had a full staff, but that in fact half my staff was on embarkation leave, hence the battle dress. The inspector applauded the idea, and went on to ask if the section looked as it did on a normal working day. Again I spoke the truth. No, I told him, we were a little cleaner than usual, but not a great deal. The floor was polished that morning, for example, something we did less often with a short staff. He smiled, and as he left I heard him comment to the CO, "You know, it's refreshing to see a place that isn't immaculate. I now have at least an idea of what the place looks like when the men are working." I heard no more about it from either the Adjutant or the CO. I had made my point, and I think I was better able to hold my own against senior officers on the station after that small incident.

Avgas (aviation gasoline) was always transported by rail tank cars to the station siding, well away from the administration area, but within the boundaries of the station proper. The AFPs (Air Force Policemen) patrolled the area to keep it secure against civilian scroungers. (Vehicular gas was rationed, and some fools might have thought that stolen avgas, diluted, would be excellent for use in their private cars.) One day a train was shunting a few tank cars onto the station siding and an accident occurred. One of the cars ruptured and gas spilled out. Somehow or other it ignited, and flames burst out abruptly. The station fire department was there in seconds, but it would take some minutes to put out the fire, and in the meantime there was the grim possibility of a terrible explosion, one that could flatten the station and cause tremendous casualties. The burning tank car was the only one hooked up to the engine, so the train began pulling slowly away in an effort to get that car away from the others. The AFP sergeant there at the time climbed aboard the flaming tank car, and when it was well away from the others, uncoupled it, jumped onto the engine, and was whisked away. The firefighters took over, quickly cooling down the tanker and dousing the fire. The sergeant suffered a few small burns for his heroic deed, but was otherwise unharmed. He was royally treated at the mess that evening, and the subject was relegated to the back of everyone's mind. A month or so later, he was awarded the George Cross. Now that's something to remember!

Another fire situation, while G/C Man was still CO, ended less happily. A fire broke out in a hangar, and the hangar was completely destroyed. Fortunately, no aircraft were lost, and the shops in the adjacent lean-tos were empty. It could have been much worse, but, nonetheless, the loss of a hangar was considerable.

When the station command was to be passed over to W/C Garb, the preparations included an inventory check. Now, someone had forgotten to write off that hangar before the Board of Inquiry concerning the fire had retired. The hangar was still on station inventory, though there was only a patch of concrete to show for it. True, it was only a paper error which could have been corrected by going through several rolls of red tape, but this would take weeks. The command change was approaching rapidly, and it was both embarrassing and a bit unfair to saddle the new CO with such a substantial inventory error. The problem had to be resolved immediately; the question of the day was how.

No. 3 Bombing and Gunnery School 73

In the services, there are three kinds of stores (supplies). "A" class includes major items such as aircraft, radios, buildings, and so forth, which all must be fully accounted for. "B" class stores include the smaller components of "A" class plus other minor items, but a station was still accountable for these. "C" class items included such things as paper clips, pens, wires, and batteries. The station did not have to account for these, though they were watched for abuse and over-consumption.

Some smart supply type came up with a simple solution to the problem of the missing hangar. An E52 was a conversion voucher, used when a number of small items were put together to form a larger item. For example, an aircrew helmet, two headphones, a microphone, a cord, and a Plug 58 became a headset when assembled. With the E52 completed, the relevant inventory then showed a reduction of the components and an addition of the assembly—quite simple and straightforward. Well, this supply type wrote up an E52 for the hangar. On the "delete from inventory" side, he typed "Hangar, Aircraft, Type —; on the "add to inventory" side, he typed "Hangers, Clothes". The simple change of a vowel converted an "A" class item to a "C" class item for which no records had to be kept. The hangar was thus written off and the command change took place without embarrassment. Tricky? Yes, but all in a good cause. I don't suppose it would get by the eyes of an auditor very easily, though.

The rooms Es and I rented when we returned from my unsuccessful stint at Clinton were by far the best we had ever had. Fully furnished, our little flat contained a bedroom, a combination living room/dining room, a kitchen, and our own bathroom. It was the second floor of a rather nice little house, and though we did use a common entrance, we still had much more privacy than previously. I had the opportunity to put in a lot more time studying, which was not something I have ever been fond of, but when you must . . . well, you manage. I had a lot of cramming to do if I was ever to pass that radar course, and we were happy to have the good fortune to be in a position where it was possible.

Another circumstance that gave me more time for studying was the appointment of a repatriated aircrew officer, a WAG I believe, to the wireless section as a signals officer. He was appointed while I was away, and as signals officer, was my senior. The only experience he had was operating a piece of equipment in an aircraft, but the

74   The War Years

Station Adjutant recommended that I go along with him as my senior, let him make his own errors, and the station would find out if he could cut the mustard as a signals officer. I suppose his lack of knowledge about the many types of equipment we had to handle had nothing to do with his ability to manage men and give priorities to work. I had been taught that a good commander never ordered anyone to do anything he could not himself do better or faster, but apparently that policy had gone out the window somewhere along the line. In any case, his appointment gave me the opportunity to concentrate on my studies.

At about that time, as well, a number of WDs (personnel from the RCAF's Women's Division) were posted in. These women were to take over the wireless operator chores in the control tower, freeing sorely needed men for our section. At first, we thought this was great, but we hadn't realized that problems were lying in wait. The control tower stairwells were open, that is, they had the treads only, with no risers. The new WDs insisted that the station put in risers in deference to their modesty. (At this time, the RCAF did not supply WDs with slacks, only skirts.) Further, the tower contained only two washrooms, one for men and one for male officers. With the arrival of the WDs, officers and men had to use one washroom, and the other had to be modified for use by the women. There were only three WDs at that time, and the administrative staff began to

WD officers inspect our ground station.

No. 3 Bombing and Gunnery School 75

wonder if all the bother was really worth the extra help in the tower. Then the WDs came up with yet another complaint. The operators had been positioned so that they faced the runways and could fully relate to the situation. For some reason, the WDs decided that they wanted to face into the building, and thus they would require modesty panels on the operating desks. It seemed like a lot of unnecessary work, but it was done.

I did believe that the WDs were doing their bit, but I also thought they should consider that it was a training base during wartime, and do their best to fit in as easily as possible. The whole mess was quickly straightened out during a visit from some senior officers of the Women's Division. If the WDs didn't shape up, they would be shipped out; a place could be found for them elsewhere. After that, there were no further problems. We soon had WDs in the supply section, the mess, the hospital, the orderly room, the safety equipment section, the accounts section, and the photo section. A queen bee was placed in charge of all WDs on the station to keep things running smoothly. (A queen bee was the senior WD officer on a station. She was usually employed in an administrative capacity.)

Like all RCAF flying stations, we had our share of crashes, but, fortunately, there were very few fatalities. One crash I will never forget took place in early summer, when a drogue ship was abandoned just before it crashed near the lake under our firing range. Apparently it was preparing to head back to base, and the pilot banked just as the drogue operator was releasing his drogue prior to winding in the cable. The drogue cleared, but for some reason the cable fouled and could neither be wound in nor released. The fouled cable became twisted about the tail assembly, and the balance of the cable, pulled taut inside the aircraft, set off a good many sparks. A small fire resulted, the drogue operator advised the pilot, and the pilot ordered a bail-out. (An aside: it was a standing order that a bail-out not be ordered on intercom, so that only the crew of that aircraft could hear it, but rather on radio, so that any aircraft in the vicinity would hear the order and be aware of the dangerous situation. It allowed other aircrew to keep an eye open for the position of the crew who bailed out. Furthermore, the ground station at the tower would hear the order and be able to set in motion any necessary emergency procedures.) The bail-out was ordered on radio, as specified, and the pilot and drogue operator made a successful jump.

I was with the vehicle that picked them up shortly afterward, and was quite astonished to see that they were both in their stocking-feet. Neither of them knew where their boots were, but a brief search located the operator's boots about a hundred yards away from where he had landed, side by side and upright in the mud. The operator's inner boots were still fully laced and inside the flight boots, which were still zipped up. The pilot's boots were found in much the same

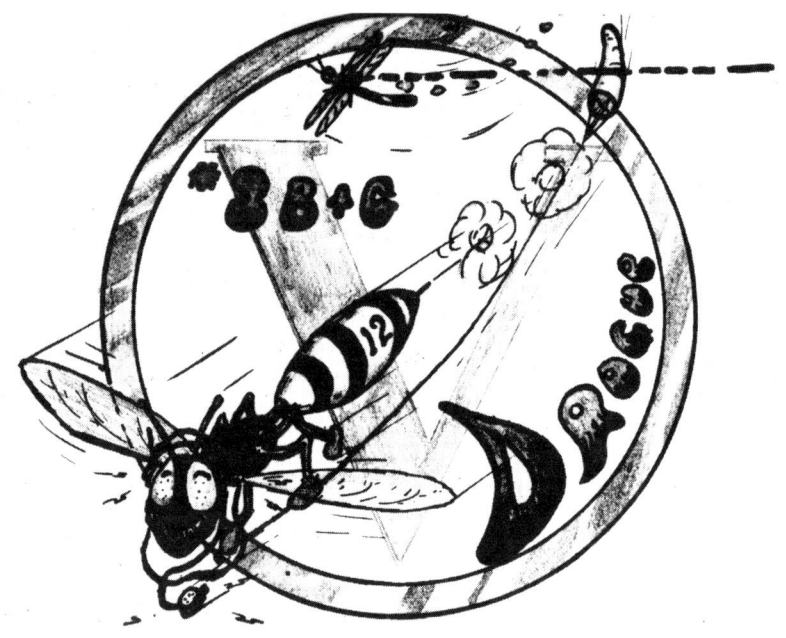

The crest of Corporal J.M.F. Marshall.

condition. We concluded that the two men must have been fully relaxed when the chutes opened, and the abrupt lessening of speed in their descent was sufficient to jerk off their boots. I imagine this would not have happened had the two men been less sure of the operation of their parachutes!

In the fall of 1944 we heard rumours of a near strike by some of the instructors at the nearby No. 3 Wireless School in Winnipeg. A strike was unheard of in the RCAF, and sounded doubly ridiculous while we were at war, so the rumours were treated as a joke and glossed over. But shortly afterward there were a lot of transfers in and out of No. 3 WS, and I was one of the victims. I was to be sent there, perhaps for just a short time. I wasn't very happy to have been involved in whatever problem No. 3 WS was having, but I wasn't given any choice. On the appointed day, I handed my inventory over to the WAG, who had assumed most of my duties, and arranged with one of the locals who owned a panel truck to move our effects from Portage to Winnipeg. And so we were on our way.

4
No. 3 Wireless School, Winnipeg
October 1944 - December 1944

I WAS TRANSFERRED TO NO. 3 Wireless School in mid-October 1944. Es and I travelled to Winnipeg a week or so prior to the reporting date to look for decent rooms. Strangely enough, the rooms we settled on were in the home of an ambassador (or was it the attaché to the ambassador?) of some occupied European country. Our rooms were on the second floor, and the bed/sitting room was not attached to the kitchen/dining room. We had bathroom privileges, which meant that we didn't have our own bathroom, but were allowed to use the household's, a common arrangement. All in all, we were pleased with what we had found.

Having paid the deposit on our rooms, I went to the wireless school to find out, if I could, what my specific job was to be. "Line instructor," I was told, "working out at Stevenson Field." As I had no idea what a line instructor might do, I wasn't much further ahead, but my informant seemed disinclined to give more details. (Stevenson Field later became the Winnipeg International Airport. I visited the airport in 1984, finding little resemblance to the field as I knew it during the war years. Then, it was a busy military airport, with a few civil flights. Now, it is a heavily used international terminal, with flights of a multitude of civil airlines arriving and departing in rapid succession. A few pictures of No. 3 WS are exhibited on the terminal's second floor, along with a tribute to Captain Stevenson, but there is nothing else to remind visitors of its wartime role.)

Back at Macdonald, Es and I packed up our belongings and prepared to move. I had accumulated a small amount of communications equipment by that time, on which Es listened to the aircraft in use. (She had listened in on the Wrong Way Corrigan episode, for one.) As well, it enabled us to hear the music we wanted, rather than that forced upon us by the local broadcasters. Most short wave receivers were in very short supply, but I had managed to assemble an impressive piece of gear that was functional and effective. We crated it carefully for its move.

We moved into our new quarters on a weekend. There was a scream from our new landlady when she saw the crate that held my precious communications equipment, but she didn't throw us out. She muttered about it, but that was to be expected. (I don't believe that it was her idea to let us stay, but the diplomat's. He had the European respect of the military, and talked her out of her desire to get rid of me.) We managed to completely settle in that weekend, even filling our cupboards with groceries and learning something about the Winnipeg streetcar and bus service. Bright and early Monday morning, I reported for duty at the wireless school.

A line instructor proved to be a briefer and debriefer for aircrew students. No. 3 WS trained wireless air gunners, or WAGs. Once they graduated and were shipped overseas, the WAGs main responsibility would be to operate the radios in bomber aircraft, though they must also be prepared to take over duties as gunners when required. Their courses at No. 3 WS included use of the radio equipment to the best advantage under any circumstances, navigation with the aircraft's radio direction-finding gear, communication with other aircraft with both voice and Morse code, and emergency repairs of the gear.

The students at No. 3 WS had received some previous gunnery training, and on completion of their wireless course, they would return to a B&GS. Nonetheless, their prime function would be the operation of the wireless equipment—manning the guns would be secondary—so the training at No. 3 WS was thorough. It included both ground school and flight training, the latter consisting of a number of exercises to prepare the WAGs for service overseas. Prior to a student's air exercise, the line instructor would detail the requirements and purpose of that specific exercise, as laid down in the course curriculum. When the pilot returned the student to the ground, the line instructor would analyse the student's performance and discuss possible improvements.

Before I did any briefing or debriefing, I had to complete two full exercises myself, to see if I was capable of judging a student's performance. I didn't have the ground school, of course, but I did receive the same pre-exercise briefings as the students. The pilot who took me up was given to believe that I was simply another student, so there would be no unfair influence, either for or against me, in the

80 *The War Years*

exercise. I made the grade without difficulty, reassuring my superiors that I could handle the job and myself that the students should be able to complete the exercises. I enjoyed the exercises, and looked forward to the days ahead.

Naturally, there were those students who, like myself, couldn't accustom themselves to the motion of the aircraft. Others found the smell of the heated oil nauseating. Yet, most of these hardy souls

The wireless radio installation in a Harvard trainer.

persevered despite their internal discomfort, graduating from the class to eventually serve overseas. I'm afraid that I hadn't, and still haven't, that sort of courage.

Other students lay on the other side of the scale, explaining that their equipment had indeed checked out okay on the ground, but had all sorts of problems as soon as airborne. It was odd how they went through the entire exercise before reporting that the gear was unserviceable. Why hadn't the student reported to the pilot as soon as the problem occurred, so they could return to base and complete the exercise in another aircraft? I listened to a variety of excuses in response to that last question. Fortunately, it was usually possible to spot which students were slackers, and their antics were soon nipped in the bud.

At least four times I did have to take a flight to check on the operation of some piece of equipment. Usually, I found that the repairs should have been well within the capability of the student and could have been effected with little loss of exercise time. Yet to hear the student tell the tale, one would think the problem far too complex to be cleared by him. If so complex, I would often wonder aloud, how was it that only ten or fifteen percent of the class found that type of problem so difficult? Almost every possible problem was gone over in detail in ground classes, and all these men had been through ITS and were supposedly similar in character, education and desire. Enough said!

No. 3 WS used Yales and Harvards, and it was my impression that the pilots enjoyed flying for the exercises. Across Stevenson Field was an AOS, or perhaps it was an ANS, and the circuit was always busy with Ansons, Yales, and Harvards all awaiting their turn to land. My students' debriefings could usually be completed just in time for us to grab a hasty lunch. Then I would brief the next group, wait out their exercises in case a problem reared its head, debrief the students on their return, and hop a bus for home. It sounds like an active, interesting day, but during my short stay at No. 3 WS, I found the days tedious and routine.

While I became accustomed to the boredom of my new job, Es was having a great time learning more about Winnipeg. She had met the sister of one of our previous landladies, and the two of them did the town! At least, they "did the town" as far as that was possible on a serviceman's salary, in Winnipeg, in wartime! Es's friendship meant that we were not completely on our own in Winnipeg.

A No. 3 WS Harvard on an exercise near Winnipeg.

In my spare time, I often liked to browse through the wares of wholesale electrical parts distributors in Winnipeg, looking for any part that might improve my communications equipment. Who was to know but that I might pick up a piece that would allow us to hear the BBC direct! One evening in early December I was chatting with the salesman at such a wholesale store when he mentioned a repair shop that had lost its serviceman. The shop was near where Es and I were living, so I asked the salesman to call the dealer and arrange an introduction.

At the repair shop, the owner seemed pleased to meet me. He had a heavy backlog of radio repairs to be done, but with no one but himself to work on them, he knew he would be unable to get the sets back to the owners for Christmas. We came rapidly to an agreement. I would come in on the weekends to help him out, being paid on a piece-work basis. He had all the necessary tools and equipment, so I figured it would be an easy way to make a few bucks to get Es a nice Christmas present. It turned out that most of the repairs were quite simple. By the second weekend, I had cleared his shop of repairs. Delighted, the owner said there were another 20 or 30 sets on hold. If I wished, he could call them in; if I stuck to doing just the repairs and let him re-assemble the sets, there was a good chance we could get them all done in time for Christmas. His customers would be pleased, and both he and I would make a bit of money. We struck a deal, and got busy.

When all the sets had been repaired, the cheque I received was much better than I had expected. Not only that, but Es and I were invited to attend a Christmas party with the owner and his wife. It was a marvelous party, and there was an unexpected bonus. One of the other guests was the owner of a private broadcasting station in Winnipeg. He assured me that when the war was over, there would be a place for me at his station if I wanted it. The radio engineer who had worked for him before the war was a signals officer with the RCAF. He planned to return to the station after the war, but the owner had decided that the amount of work justified the hiring of an assistant. Naturally, I was delighted to receive such an offer.

About a week prior to Christmas, the No. 3 WS Orderly Room told me I would be transferred to No. 15 SFTS (Service Flying Training School) in Claresholm, Alberta. I was to report no later than January 5th, 1945. During the last week of December, Es and I arranged to have our various bits and pieces picked up and taken to the express sheds to await shipment by rail to Claresholm. We bought Es a ticket and used a transport warrant to obtain mine. By the last day of 1944, we had cleared No. 3 WS. After just ten weeks in Winnipeg, we were on our way once more.

5
No. 15 Service Flying Training School Claresholm, Alberta
January 1945 - February 1945

WE TOOK THE TRAIN FROM WINNIPEG on New Year's Eve, arriving in Calgary on January 2nd, 1945. Claresholm was south of Calgary, near the foothills of the Rockies, so we were to make a connection in Calgary for the southbound train. Es had developed a severe cold by this time, and when several ladies from the Red Cross met us at the station in Calgary, nothing would have it but that we accompany one of them to their nearby hostel, where Es could lie down. There was some talk of calling in a doctor, but after Es had rested for a time she felt better, and even well enough to continue with our trip. We made it back to the station with nearly half an hour to spare before our train left.

The scenery on our journey south to Claresholm was beautiful, with the towering Rockies dominating the skyline. The foothills, clothed in evergreens and draped with white snow, with the limitless shadings of silvery grey and warm brown rock peering through, were breathtaking, and quite enough to take Es out of her misery. We arrived at Claresholm in the late afternoon, and were surprised that no servicewives' committee was there to meet us. On our own, we sought and found the only hotel in town, registered, had supper, and took to bed early, exhausted by our long hours on the train.

A loud party going on in the hotel's bar was powerless to disturb our sleep, until a scratching noise at our door woke me at about two or three in the morning. The sound of a key unlocking the door was followed by stealthy footsteps as someone entered our room and made his way to the dresser. Now fully awake, I prepared to leap out of bed as soon as the intruder laid a hand on any of our possessions. He touched nothing but the two clean hotel glasses, which he quickly spirited off to the party still going on downstairs. After re-locking the door hastily, I left the key in the door to ensure privacy, jammed a chair beneath the doorknob, and returned to bed to pass the rest of the night in an uneasy sleep.

Before breakfast the next morning I spoke with the desk clerk about our nocturnal visitor, and was appalled by the casual way he shrugged the incident off. As nothing of ours had been taken, he couldn't see that any harm had been done. This was the only hotel in town, so Es and I had little choice but to live with that irresponsible attitude, but needless to say we were determined to find other lodgings as soon as we could. As I left for the station, Es, whose health had much improved, was preparing for a day of apartment-hunting.

The routine of checking in at a new station was old hat to me by this time, and there was nothing unusual about that routine at No. 15 SFTS. I was given a check-in slip and a map of the station, and assured that it was acceptable to live off the station, as there was a shortage of senior NCO's quarters. I visited the various departments to announce my arrival and ensure that I was properly recorded everywhere—accounts, supply, CE, ME, hospital, dentist, AFP, photo section, etc. The wireless section was my last point of call, as I wanted to get a thorough look at the whole station before checking in at my own section. One thing I learned from my travels was the importance of radios at this station. As an SFTS, No. 15 required a radio in almost every aircraft. It was the final training centre for pilots before their postings overseas, and radios were a vital piece of equipment. Whatever my responsibilities were to be, and I had the idea that I would be supervising repairs in the wireless section, my position would surely be one of some importance.

The first person I spoke with in the wireless section was the flight sergeant I had been sent to replace. His posting out had been cancelled, and he had absolutely no desire to hand over his job to someone else. He suggested that I check with the Signals Officer to determine my exact status.

The situation turned out to be the same as that at Macdonald. A repatriated air officer was filling the boots of Signals Officer, but this one wasn't even slightly acquainted with the trade! A pilot who had served his tour overseas and come home with a few ribbons, he no doubt deserved a less arduous job, but, I thought, of all things why wireless? A half-hour's conversation answered my question. The Air Force recognized that the technical trades associated with aviation were increasing in importance. After the war, repatriated aircrew were to be offered the chance to be put through college or university to get a degree in one of these trades, courtesy of the Air Force, on the condition that they then come back into the RCAF as Technical Officers. This particular pilot had decided that wireless was the up and coming field, and had chosen to take the Air Force up on their offer, hence his posting as Signals Officer in charge of a wireless section on an SFTS. As I had no aspirations toward becoming an officer (note: I am not referring to the rank of warrant officer), I felt no personal threat at the thought of all these inexperienced men serving as officers in the various trades, but I did consider it a mistake on the part of the Air Force. In any event, this Signals Officer promised to discuss my position at No. 15 SFTS with the higher authorities and get back to me as soon as I was settled.

Meanwhile, Es was having her share of amusement in Claresholm. The local paper had provided few possibilities for lodgings, so she visited the office of a real estate agent to enquire about furnished houses to rent. It seemed unlikely that a town as small as Claresholm would have any such house available, but at least the agent might be able to offer some suggestions on other avenues to pursue. Will wonders never cease, the agent actually had a furnished house listed to rent. The mayor of Claresholm, a widower, had died not long before, and his house was available. Family members from a nearby town had removed his personal effects, but the furnishings remained. Would Es and I care to have a look at it? Most assuredly we would. Es made arrangements for us to meet the agent late that afternoon to view the house, and returned to the hotel.

While at the station, I had learned many details of the housing situation in Claresholm from other servicemen who lived out. After Es told me of her good fortune in locating a house, I briefed her on my findings. Few houses in Claresholm had indoor bathrooms. Heating was by gas. Basements were rare, and houses could be felt to shift on their foundations early in the mornings as the temperature changed. Most houses did have running water, with a septic system for grey water (dishwater, etc.), and there was a honey pail outfit for cleaning out the outhouse. It was a situation to which Es and I had not yet been subjected, but none of the nearby towns were any better, and at least the rents were reasonable.

The real estate agent treated us to dinner before taking us to the house in question. Despite the forewarnings of the housing situation, I was a little surprised by what we found—after all, this had been the home of the mayor. Unpainted, the small, two-storey house had a kitchen and living room on the ground floor and two bedrooms, with a few closets, upstairs. A summer kitchen, or shed, was attached at the back of the house, and that was all there was to it. It was all furnished, as promised, but little more than that. The only sink was in the kitchen, which also had a gas stove, as expected, and in the living room was the gas-fired space heater. A well travelled path led from the summer kitchen to the outhouse, some fifty feet or so to the rear of the house. It was about eight in the evening and black as the ace of spades, but rather than take the chance of losing our prize by waiting to see it in daylight, we signed a deal with the real estate agent immediately. Our rental of the place was subject to our being transferred or posted out; that is, if I were moved to another station before our rental agreement ran out, we were not to be penalized with an extra month's rent or anything.

We returned to the hotel for our second and last night there, which passed uneventfully. The next morning I suggested that Es contact the rail express people about our effects (she had already picked up our cat the previous day), so we could move into our new house as soon as possible. She agreed, but added that no matter what, she would have checked us out of the hotel and have our hand baggage moved by taxi by the time I came home that evening. I was NOT to have supper at the station, as she would have it ready for me at the house. It would be a hectic day for her, and as I left for No. 15, she began her self-appointed duties.

The Signals Officer had indeed discussed my disposition with the Brass. I was to conduct some ground school classes (my course at the School of Pedagogy was no doubt responsible for this) and to be seconded to the Signals Officer, to advise him on the various duties for which he would be responsible. In other words, I was to teach him his job, one I obviously knew and could have handled, but which he was to be spoon-fed so that he might get the glory (such as it was). Well, if that was to be my job, I decided that I might as well make the best of it. I arranged to have some furniture for myself moved into his office, got the necessary books from the Station Educational Officer, and arranged a schedule that would allow me to prepare and teach my ground school lessons, cram for the course at Clinton, and lead the would-be Signals Officer through the details of his job.

I had nothing against this individual pilot, but I could not but believe that there was a problem with such a system. I considered it a mistake for the Air Force to have promised repatriates jobs for which they were in no way qualified in skill, temperament, or ability. My particular trainee had been in his first year of agricultural studies when he enlisted. He had no intention of abandoning his previously intended vocation. When the war was over, he would go back to get his degree in that course, before returning to the RCAF to take advantage of the Air Force's offer. With the second, fully paid-for course under his belt, he would become a qualified Signals Officer! His plan was not unique. The other repatriates I met on the station had similar ideas. None of them felt a commitment for their planned RCAF career. All intended to complete studies in their originally planned education before taking the RCAF courses, so they would have a cushion in the event that they didn't make it in the Air Force, or didn't like it, or the Air Force changed its plans. Now, perhaps the repatriates had reason for that way of doing things, but it didn't strike me as a good attitude to take in starting a new career, particularly when the RCAF was offering such a generous start.

When I went home to our new house that night, Es had a delicious dinner ready, and over our meal she regaled me with the stories of other service wives. There were not many staff living in town, and of course the best houses had been taken by officers, who had more money to spend and who passed their houses to other officers as they were posted in and out. One sergeant and his wife were living in a converted chicken coop. It was clean and had been thoroughly disinfected, but it was, nevertheless, a converted chicken coop! Others had houses similar to ours, but none had running water, as we did. Also, apologies had been extended to Es for the lack of any welcoming committee attending our arrival. The woman who normally telephoned the orderly room to check on incoming staff had been ill that day, and thus we had been missed.

Es sympathized with me when I told her of my new job. We agreed that as soon as I considered myself ready, I should arrange to return for the course at Clinton. Perhaps things would then look up and I would again have a section to run. I wasn't entirely optimistic, and after what I had learned that day, I had some serious reservations about my post-war career in the RCAF. One of the uninterested repatriates could well be my boss after the war, and it wouldn't be a situation I could easily stomach. But for now, there was still a war on, and my contribution would continue to be an honest one.

My work at the station rapidly became a tedious routine. My one lecture daily was attended by my trainee, as well as the class concerned. I spent at least three hours cracking the books to cram for the Clinton course, and the balance of the day went into showing the Signals Officer the ropes. For a short while I was in charge of the section while the flight sergeant I had originally been sent to replace was on leave. I became accustomed to the sight of the station's Harvards overhead, as well as the few Ansons and Yales. Nearly all the station's aircraft had radios, backed up with an additional intercom amplifier. In the event of a radio failure, there would still be an intercom for essential inter-crew communication.

A flight of Harvards in formation over Claresholm, Alberta.

Parades, of course, were a fact on life on the station, but there is one wings parade I will never forget. (In wings parades, the graduating students were presented with their pilots' wings or their gunners', observers', or navigators' half-wings, usually by some visiting dignitary. The graduates wore this badge of office with deserved pride.) For this parade I had been taken off my usual job and been allocated the job of Squadron Warrant Officer, which meant, among other things, that my position during the ceremony would be close to the podium. Such a change was not unusual, and I thought little of it until my name was called at the end of the ceremony. Startled, I nonetheless walked up onto the podium, to be awarded the Efficiency Medal for my combined service in the Army and Air Force. I had made application for this award without expecting anything to come of it, for though such medals had been given in the Army, I knew of none ever being awarded in the RCAF. My only regret was not knowing of the award in advance so that Es might have been there. Like most of the staff, I had already received the Canadian Volunteer Service Medal, so now I was wearing two gongs, or at least the ribbons. The unusual green and yellow ribbon of the Efficiency Medal attracted more than a little attention.

While I slogged through the routine of my days at the station, Es was becoming acquainted with other service wives in Claresholm. One afternoon while a friend was visiting, she and Es decided to continue their conversation over a coffee at the hotel coffee bar. Es pulled on her baby sealskin coat and began searching through the pockets for her gloves. (I had bought the coat with some of the buckshee dollars earned fixing radios in Winnipeg. Such a coat would have been impossible on my service wages.) Patting one pocket, she felt something move, and knew instantly what it must be. After sending the squeamish friend into the other room on some pretext, Es picked up our cat and popped its head into her pocket. The cat needed no prompting to make a hasty snack of the mouse, for such it was, and Es and her friend left for the hotel. Es and I often thought that Claresholm should have been renamed Mouse Town; there was a regular parade of the little creatures through our house. As the house shifted on its foundation every now and again, a half-inch wide crack would appear between the plate of the house and the walls. This we stuffed with paper to keep out the weather, but paper didn't deter the mice. Fortunately, our cat developed a taste for them, and as the house settled again all would be well . . . till the next time.

A small joke in Claresholm was the Saturday evening bath ritual. Every house had a large copper or tin tub, which every Saturday would be placed in front of the gas heater and filled with hot water, so the lady of the house could take a bath. (The gentlemen had their baths at the station.) Even on the coldest of Saturday evenings, no service couple would walk into the house of another without both a firm invitation and assurances that bath-time had come and gone. Unexpected guests could have been most embarrassing!

Then there were the chinooks. These winds are the wonder of the foothills. Leaving for work on a crisp January morning, I would find that my greatcoat was a must, as the temperature was usually well below freezing, and sometimes below $0°F$. By mid-morning, the chinook would have blown in, any snow would have melted, the air would be balmy, and I would wonder how I could have needed a greatcoat just a few hours before!

Food was never scarce, but some items were in short supply. The common commodities—icing sugar, brown sugar, jelly powder and other sugar products, butter, and meat—were rationed. Other items, such as raisins, tea, and even coffee, were usually available, but sometimes one had to wait for them. (There was no "serve yourself" routine then, such as at today's supermarkets. All the grocers, even branches of national chains, had counter service. You asked the clerk for what you wanted, and he packed it, totalled the bill, and either sent it on to your home by delivery boy or, if you were fortunate enough to own a car, have it carried out for you. It seems to me they were more careful then with perishables and delicate items, such as eggs, placing them on top of the parcel rather than under the cans, as I often think is the bent today! If the clerk didn't like the cut of your jib, you might not get the raisins or tea you really wanted. They weren't after tips or anything, simply a pleasant word and a thank-you. We service people responded with the occasional pass to a station entertainment, or some such thing. All in all, we found it an agreeable way of life.)

One day while Es was putting out the garbage, she noticed a neighbour burning some trash. The garbage-man was due just the next day, so Es's curiosity got the better of her and she asked the neighbour about it. With an embarrassed grin, the woman replied that she would have been ashamed to have it been seen in the garbage. A few months earlier she had sent her children to the store for about ten pounds of then scarce raisins. Hoarding them against the day she might need them, she hadn't noticed when they became wormy. She had just looked them up that morning, discovered they were bad, and decided to burn them so no one else would know of the waste.

There was very little social life in Claresholm, or at least, Es and I were not aware of any. We took in all the station movies, but I spent much of my spare time studying. I don't recall whether there was a theatre in town—if there was, it certainly didn't leave any impression on either of us. It wasn't long before we agreed that the time we were spending in Claresholm was neither useful nor enjoyable. My mind felt saturated with studying, and my books became a bore. My work at the station was nothing more than a routine, and no longer seemed to have much value. In mid-spring, unwilling to wait till the Air Force found me a more interesting posting, I went to the station orderly room for details of the courses that were running at Clinton. I was met with a blank stare. Where was Clinton? What courses was I talking about? and so on. Through the good graces of the trainee I had so generously dedicated some considerable time to, I was granted an interview with the Station Adjutant, who agreed to signal Clinton to determine just where I stood with that course I was muttering about. The reply came back in a few days: a course was to commence in early May. It was suggested that No. 15 SFTS signal Ottawa DAPS, mention that I was supernumary to their establishment and that I wished to take the WM R course at Clinton, and perhaps DAPS would see fit to effect the necessary transfer. DAPS was promptly affirmative, and I cleared No. 15 SFTS and prepared to ship off to No. 5 Radio School, Clinton, on course once more.

My trainee officer was sorry to see me leave, but hoped we would meet again within the next few years, as he was determined to make it as a Signals Officer. He made it clear that I had shown him the career possibilities in the wireless trade. He no longer planned to complete his agricultural studies, but instead would attempt a course to further him in his RCAF career. I was enormously pleased to hear that, and actually looked forward to seeing him again. Perhaps we would both benefit from those months spent together at Claresholm.

Es and I packed up our belongings once more and shipped them off, but not to Clinton. We thought it likely that there would soon be a Pacific force called for, and as I had not been sent to the Atlantic or European campaign, it seemed logical to believe that I might be going to the Pacific after completing my course at Clinton. Also, during the six-week course it would probably be best for my studies if I lived at the station, rather than travelling home every night to entertain and be entertained by Es! At the same time, Es was eager to resume her music and piano teaching, and it would be best for her to live in an area where there would be many potential pupils, rare at a service base. So Es was to live in St. Catharines, Ontario, while I studied, and quite possibly after that should I be sent overseas. We chose that city because my folks lived there at the time, so Es could at least have a roof over her head should it be difficult to find a good location for her studio.

I had about a week's leave coming, and adding my travel time and a scrounged weekend or two, I was able to accompany Es to St. Catharines. We found a place and moved her in before I had to report to Clinton. Es was established; I was on course and knew what I had to face; I was prepared for it; and I had no worries. I felt I could take that course now, hands down!

6
No. 5 Radio School, Clinton, Ontario
March 1945 - June 1945

I HAD NO ILLUSIONS when I arrived at Station Clinton. I knew it would be a tough six months, but was determined that I would make the course and even come out near the top end of the class. There was little change in the outward appearance of the station—it still looked like a concentration camp—but there did seem to be a change of attitude.

I was allotted a room in the Senior NCOs' quarters, which were adjacent to the Sergeants' Mess. The quarters were in a two-storey H-hut with two to a room. My room was on the upper floor, which, fortunately, meant that I would hear little if any noise. It was well away from the washrooms in the central cross-bar of the H, which again meant less noise, and was on the outside edge of the building. It was perhaps not the most convenient of locations, but for my purpose—quiet, uninterrupted study—it was ideal.

I met the rest of the course students over lunch. We learned that we would be divided into two parts for lessons in theory, but would participate together in the practical classes. To my surprise, F/S Unit (now a WO2) was also taking the course; he would be in WM R 8(a), and I in WM R 8(b). (F/S Unit, you will recall, was the wireless section flight sergeant when I arrived in Macdonald, Manitoba.) My section of the course, B, included four flight sergeants, two sergeants, and three corporals, quite a mix. The other class was equally mixed in rank, but some of those students were radar techs on conversion. Their problems, we assumed, would lie with the communications portion of the course, just as we wireless types would have trouble with the radar.

The CI was W/C Rogers, the same officer who had okayed my earlier resignation from the course while recommending that I some-day return. He made it clear to all and sundry that this course represented the new Air Force. We might as well dig in and get our feet wet, as there would be no room for slackers and work dodgers. It was up to us to learn what we could, to get the course under our belts, so we could remain useful to the Air Force of the future.

The course was quite as difficult as I had expected and required considerable effort on the part of the students, both radar and communications. Some of the class results are appended, and they indicate how little relation there was between rank and scholastic standing. It turned out to be to our advantage to have two theory instructors. If one instructor's presentation was unclear, a student could sit in on the other instructor's class, and he might put the subject in a different way. A more thorough understanding was thus possible. As before, we were not allowed to remove our notebooks from the compound. At first, this seemed to result in little more than endless weary hours in the classroom, studying under supervision, but it proved to be yet another asset. As our instructors soon tired of the constant association with us, they prevailed on other instructors to exchange classes for supervised study. We were then able to learn other methods and points of view, and, I think, received a clearer picture as a result. Finally, we would often argue points of theory in the barracks, and many of us believed that these discussions were responsible for the good marks we finally achieved.

WM R 8(b). The author is in the front row, second from the left.

ASG, 4 May 1945

FS	Velleman	Above Average
FS	MacKay	Average
Cpl	Preston	( )
Cpl	Goodwill	( )
FS	McKenna	Below Average
Sgt	Chapman	( )
FS	Knight	( )
Sgt	Ford	( )
Cpl	Moore	( )

Class Average: 60 percent

ABK/F, 15 May 1945

FS	Velleman	Above Average
Sgt	Chapman	Average
FS	Knight	( )
Cpl	Goodwill	( )
FS	MacKay	( )
Cpl	Preston	( )
FS	McKenna	( )
Sgt	Moore	( )
Sgt	Ford	( )

Class Average: 69 percent

SCR 729, 16 May 1945

FS	Velleman	Above Average
Cpl	Goodwill	( )
Sgt	Chapman	( )
FS	MacKay	Average
Cpl	Preston	( )
FS	Knight	( )
FS	McKenna	( )
Sgt	Ford	( )
Cpl	Moore	( )

Class Average: 68.6 percent

LRN/AYF, 26 May 1945

Cpl	Preston	Average
FS	Velleman	( )
FS	MacKay	( )
Cpl	Goodwill	( )
FS	McKenna	( )
FS	Knight	( )
Sgt	Ford	Below Average
Sgt	Chapman	( )

Class Average: 65.25 percent

FM, 9 June 1945

FS	MacKay	Above Average
FS	Velleman	( )
Cpl	Goodwill	Average
Cpl	Preston	( )
Sgt	Ford	( )
FS	McKenna	( )
Sgt	Chapman	Below Average
FS	Knight	( )

Class Average: 64.5 percent

HP Transmitters, 23 June 1945

FS	Velleman	Above Average
Sgt	Chapman	( )
FS	McKenna	( )
FS	MacKay	( )
Cpl	Goodwill	( )
Sgt	Ford	( )
Cpl	Preston	Average

Class Average: 79.8 percent

Some Class Results, WM R 8(b), Clinton, Ontario

Spring in Clinton was beautiful, but the station itself was not a pretty place. It had been built over an old farm, and the silo and farmhouse were still there. The other buildings, if there had been any, had been razed. The farmhouse was being used as a sort of supply room. Entry to the station was off the highway between Clinton and London. A guardhouse stood beside the electrically operated barrier, and across from the guardhouse was the hostess house, a small building where airmen could visit with their relatives if the airmen were unable to leave the station. (Earlier in the war, students at the then RAF-operated school and station were not permitted to leave the station during certain periods of their course.) It was a comfortable little house with several living rooms. The hostesses, local volunteers and personnel from the Red Cross and the Sally Ann, served tea and coffee, and the atmosphere was congenial.

On the station road just north of the entrance was the orderly room, and to the south were the Officers' Mess and quarters, the dental clinic, and the station hospital. Further east on the same road was the parade square, an acre and a half of paved asphalt.

Directly opposite the doorway of the the station orderly room was a small attention area, where the flag pole stood. The flag pole was the standard RCAF type, with a yardarm supporting the RCAF ensign and the CO's residency flag at the top of the pole. The CO's flag was much like a small ensign in appearance, but with the Union Jack replaced with bars indicating the resident CO's rank. Very pukka, very service.

The parade square could be crossed to gain entry to the senior NCO's barracks and the fire hall, but one then had to cross the attention area. The other way to make access to these places was to walk around the edge of the square. The perimeter of the parade square was dotted with crabapple trees, and they were a beautiful sight at blossom time in the spring. It made the drill square a little more palatable. Trees and bushes had been planted all over the station; it is my firm belief that this was a vain attempt to overcome the concentration camp atmosphere that otherwise prevailed! The messes all had flower beds, carefully tended, and summer was the time to see Clinton at its best.

The theory portion of the course was not only difficult, but the method of its interpretation was different from what I had encountered in any other course. Apparently, that is what threw me the first time I attempted the radar course. This time I was ready for it, and the classes made much more sense. An example: in radio theory, a tube was basically an amplifier or detector; in radar, it was not only that, but was also used as a switch, something I hadn't understood before. Practical labs backed up the theory, but I was sceptical of the experiments we were given and made it my business to have a look at the backs of the practice boards. In most cases, they had been gimmicked to work according to theory. Now, theory is all well and good, but if the real product doesn't support that theory, something must be wrong with one or the other, and it doesn't make much sense if a gimmick must be used to prove the abstract idea. There is a well known saying: "The design engineer can never recognize his brainchild when it comes off the production line." This applies in most trades and particularly in the high tech field. In this case, I don't think any theorist would have recognized the results of his work in the gimmicked experiment boards.

Somehow, I managed to get to St. Catharines to see Es almost every weekend. WO2 Unit drove to Toronto in his four-door convertible every weekend to see his wife, and he liked to take along passengers to help pay for the trip. When I was one of those, he would drop me off near Hamilton, where I could catch a bus to arrive in St. Catharines before ten in the evening. Sunday evenings, I would meet WO2 Unit where he had dropped me, and we were usually back at the barracks by ten or eleven.

Es was enjoying her teaching. It took next to no time before she had enough students. The apartment was satisfactory, and she managed to sublet the unnecessary garage to someone to get back a few of the rent dollars. We had furnished it comfortably, and Es was happy there. The only fly in the ointment was our unavoidable separation; we hadn't been apart for any length of time in over three years, since she followed me to Macdonald in the fall of 1941.

The course was progressing at a merry rate; I was pleased with my standing this time. The results of the tests were published regularly, and though I wasn't at the head of the class, I was near it. I had the impression that the instructors were now much more inclined to be on our side. It was difficult for them, as the students were not all at the same level. (For the uninitiated, the level of a student is the highest point at which he is able to absorb the instruction. This naturally varies from student to student, and only a good instructor can determine whether he is teaching too far above that point. The expert instructor finds the level and teaches just above it, so the majority of the class must reach for their study goal and their interest is maintained. To teach below or too far above the proper level is to lose the class.)

Fortunately, by the time a few drop-outs had been eliminated from the course, the level became clear. By then, the basic theory classes were over and we were into the applied theory and the gimmicked practice boards. I attempted to point out to the officers in the experimental labs that the gimmicks destroyed any purpose to the experiments. How meaningful was the application of a theory to the results of a rigged experiment? I never got a satisfactory answer to that question during the entire course! None of the radar type students questioned this at all. Perhaps they had run into such things before. In any case, the applied theory experiments were eventually completed, and we moved in the equipment phase of the course.

This was the part of the course in which I found myself most comfortable. I thoroughly enjoyed troubleshooting and found to my complete surprise that I worked well with the high power equipment. The classes were interesting, and the work on the high power gear was fascinating, whether I was dealing with the simple GT20 aerodrome control transmitter, which ran about 50 watts, or the GT28, which ran 50,000 watts. Of course, there were many intermediate pieces of equipment, such as the AT3, GT24, GT27, and so forth. All pieces were heavy ground communications equipment.

Though the high power gear had struck my fancy, it appeared that there was a reluctance amongst the instructors to handle it. That may or may not have been the case, but, nonetheless, none of them seemed to feel the appeal for it that I did. I enjoyed the feeling of awe the gear gave me when it worked, and there were few of us who liked to handle it when it didn't, so I had a lot of opportunity for "hands-on" learning. The high power communications equipment was quite dissimilar to the radar gear, which had a higher rated power but a lower actual power, for it was pulsed. My fascination with the equipment is difficult to explain. Why do some mechanics like small cars, while others prefer racing cars and engines? At any rate, I made it my business to learn as much as possible about every piece of high power gear at Clinton.

The GT24 was about ten kilowatts and was a linear transmitter as far as voice communications were concerned. It used an AT3, a small, two-channel transmitter, as a driver, or exciter. The GT27 was also a ten-kilowatt unit and was used for RTT (radio teletype) or CW (continuous wave, or Morse). It had a number of channels available. The GT28 was a monstrous 50-kilowatt CW transmitter of low frequency, designed to beat through the atmosphere where all other means failed, such as in northern Canada where the aurora borealis (northern lights) could distort or destroy other radio waves. Each piece of gear had its own specific use, and each had its own peculiar problems. The AT3, though smaller than the other gear, had a complex control system. In my personal view, the instructional staff completely glossed over the complexity of the system. There were relays and delay devices in the system that were quite esoteric and were never explained. They worked, and that was all we needed to know. I was determined that if I ever became an instructor, I would right that situation!

There were many pieces of radar gear, too. The predominant ones were the airborne devices, as the only ground radars on hand were an obsolete and scrapped CH and CHL, and an AMES 11. (CH stands for Chain Home, a high-firing radar with a fixed antenna that searched for high-flying aircraft. A CHL was a similar device for low flyers. Though I didn't know what it meant at the time, I recently learned that AMES stood for Air Ministry Experimental Station. Presumably, the AMES 11 was the eleventh experiment.) The CH equipment was massive, as was the antenna tower, an impressive structure about 20 feet across at the base and 200 feet high, built of wooden timbers that had been coated with creosote to prevent rot and to slow burning. The AMES 11 was a complete and fully mobile high-power, ground-transportable radar station.

Once we had learned how to set up and use the AMES 11, plus some VHF communications gear (in this case, the SCR 641 convoy), we were ready for an exercise away from the school. The exercise was to be run over a weekend. We were to be almost completely independent of the station, with the radio communications gear as our only connection. Data on all flights observed by our radar were to be radioed to the station. A simple exercise, but the RCAF had no field kitchens, and no access to camping supplies other than the tents used in the summer by visiting air cadets.

The author in 1945 at Clinton, Ontario.

We were shipped out with our tents and little advance warning to Bayfield, a small town on the bluffs overlooking Lake Huron. In addition to our technical responsibilities, we would each have certain "housekeeping" chores, such as cooking, latrines, and so forth. Rather than get stuck with something like looking after the latrines, I volunteered as cook. I could probably do as well as anyone else in that line, and no doubt better than most. My first task was to shanghai a couple of pot scrubbers, and together we set up the best kitchen facility we could under the circumstances. My technical responsibilities were reduced, as I would be kept quite busy with the kitchen, but I was not to be totally excused. The exercise was still my prime reason for being there.

The station mess hall had done us very well. They had no way of knowing who the cook might be, had thought it might be one of themselves, and they weren't about to sell their own people short. We had almost everything one could ask for, except a good field kitchen stove. That was makeshift, but we managed. Our first meal was lunch, and we made up sandwiches and coffee and served it to everyone at their posts, so there would be a continuation of the work of setting up the tents and gear. There was a chance it might storm, and rain was the one thing that might stop the weekend exercise if it came before set-up was completed. Fortunately, the storm stayed away, and communications were established with the base without a hitch.

The meal menus were left up to me, as I had the ration list and knew what there was to eat and how many people had to be fed. As it was the first night and we would all be confined to the area, I figured it would be an ideal night for a real bang-up meal. After careful consideration of the rations, I worked out this menu:

Steaks a la Velleman
Potatoes Hashé
Vegetable en eau
Coffee, Tea, Milk
Ice Cream

There were about forty souls to feed, so the three of us were too busy to notice that the CO of the school had driven up and was prowling about. He arrived at the mess tent just as we finished setting the tables and were preparing the final touches of the meal. The gang came in and sat down, so I made my way to the CO to ask him to stay for the meal. After nodding his acceptance, the CO said that my face seemed familiar. Knowing who he was and where we had last seen each other, I asked him if he had flown any Goblins lately. W/C Hood, to whom I had last spoken when he was an F/O and the Signals Officer at Rockcliffe, remembered me then, and took the offered seat. When dinner was over and the pot-wallopers were doing their job, W/C Hood looked me up to compliment me on the meal, mentioning at the same time that he had known full well who I was without my pointed question. He also had some surprising news. My wife was in town, at the Hotel Clinton, wondering what had become of me. W/C Hood said he would drive me in for the evening, and transport would be waiting at the hotel door the next morning at 0500 to return me in time to have breakfast ready for the troops. I was more than a little surprised and impressed by Hood's readiness to put himself out so that Es and I could spend some time together.

I found Es waiting expectantly at the hotel. Apparently, when I had called earlier to tell her that I mightn't be able to make it home that weekend, we had somehow or other misunderstood each other. She had been left with the idea that she was to come to Clinton to see me, instead. Arriving in Clinton to discover that I wasn't on the station, she had naturally queried my whereabouts. The Orderly Officer, in desperation, had turned her over to the CO, W/C Hood, who arranged to meet her at the hotel before coming out to the exercise site. The two of them had had quite a chat. So much for meek service wives! Nonetheless, it was a happy treat that I was able to see her that weekend.

I was ready and waiting when transport showed up the next morning, and arrived at the site just in time to prepare breakfast before the main group got up. Two men had been on wireless and radar watch overnight, and my assistants had ensured they were well provisioned with coffee and sandwiches during their tour of duty.

That day and the next were a complete success. I enjoyed the double duty, and not having to spend the nights on camp, as the transport arrived again to whisk me away and return me at 0500. The meals were by no means posh, but were quite edible. The radar and communications facilities worked well. Some of the instructors arrived during the exercise to put faults on the gear, but these problems were quickly located and eliminated successfully. It was an excellent weekend all around.

Before leaving the weekend entirely, a final word about the AMES 11 convoy: it was complete even to an operations room. Equipped with a pair of diesels, it had all the power cabling and so forth that might ever be needed. It was a marvellous device, though not quite ahead of its time. The VHF gear used for communications was an American VHF convoy known as an SCR641. It had both a D/F (direction finding) and communications capability, and was independent of the AMES convoy even for power.

Our final exams were to be held in the first week of May, after which we would be given our postings to our new stations. The finals were not easy, but all of us were confident that we would make the grade, and indeed we did. All of us expected to be sent to Lachine or some other holding depot for possible forwarding to units being assembled for the Pacific campaign, but not so. As we were given our marks on that last Friday, we were told that postings would be released on Monday morning. No holding depot would be in store for any of us.

Relieved and happy with our passing grades on the radar course, we left the station in a hurry that evening, with our weekend passes in our pockets. We were stopped at the guardhouse with more good news. All passes had been extended to Wednesday morning at 0600 hours. Victory had been achieved in Europe. It was 8 May 1945, VE-Day!

I arrived in St. Catharines that evening in a jubilant mood. WO2 Unit and I had listened to the car radio all the way from Clinton to Hamilton to hear all about VE-Day, more than certain now that we would be shipped to some staging depot for the Pacific Campaign. Es was as excited as everyone else. The first part of the war was finally over, and perhaps it wouldn't be too long before the end of the war was in sight, too. We made no plans, and my parting words to Es the following Tuesday afternoon were that I would call her as soon as I knew where I would be going.

The Station Warrant Officer at Clinton was, as well he should be, a disciplinarian. In the past, I had seldom crossed the paths of these people, and, like most tradesmen, had little use for them. Yet this particular Warrant Officer remains vivid in my memory for the example he set. There was never a day while I was on course at

Clinton that he wasn't in the mess, asking us how we were doing and if there were any problems he could help us with. His mascot, a large, long-haired Newfoundland Labrador, was always outside the mess, on the stoop in good weather and just inside the foyer in bad. The two were inseparable, and I imagine there was a special arrangement between the SWO and the CO regarding this animal. Even on parade, this beast followed the SWO about, except when he took over the parade or was required to face the CO or parade commander. The dog seemed to know the parade orders as well as or perhaps better than most of the staff. I only regret that I didn't come to know both the man and the dog better; the next time I went to Clinton, both were gone, and so, I felt, was some of the character of the station.

There were others, too, who will remain forever in my memory. One was a WO1 S.C. James. Sidney Cyril, as we all knew him, was almost a legend in the RCAF wireless trade. Known and respected by all, he was a man of contradictions, an Old School wireless man who was nevertheless always up to date on the latest technology. He was studious, yet loved to play. An airman, he was still a WO1. While I was at Clinton on the WM R course, Sidney Cyril was the school monitor. I remember seeing him in class once, as interested and enthused by the lesson as any of the students. In my mind, he was the ideal WO. I had occasion to meet Sidney Cyril again at a later time in Clinton.

In 1983 I heard that SC James taught school in Montreal after his retirement from the RCAF, but he was dropped from this position when he didn't fit into their pension plan. He went into real estate for a time, and then did something most unusual . . . unusual, that is, for anyone but SC James. He went to theological college, graduated successfully, and is now a minister of the faith! SC James is living proof of the importance of willpower.

Other WOs play their part in my memory, but these two hold a special place in my mind. In many ways, these two men were quite similar, particularly in their dedication to their work, yet they were quite different, too. The SWO had just the manner one expected from a discip, and SC James was exactly suited to his position as a technical man. Whoever selected them for their jobs at Clinton was certainly to be complimented, for they suited their positions to a 'T'.

The Chief Instructor while I was at Clinton was W/C Rogers, an RCAF officer with a wireless background. The initial pep talk he gave us when we arrived did not impress me of itself, but I was impressed that an ex-wireless man was advising us to get the full scope of electronics, to put aside any prejudices we held for the other trade we would soon be absorbing. He would not be surprised by the achievements and great strides that have been made in the electronics industry over the past four decades.

Our new postings and transfers were given us on 13 May. After a week of leave, I was to go to No. 10 SFTS in Souris, Manitoba, which was to be used as a holding depot. Es cancelled a few classes so we could enjoy our time together before I travelled west. Mother and Dad didn't say much about my posting, but I think they were more than a bit worried about the possibility of my going to the Pacific.

7
No. 10 Service Flying Training School Souris, Manitoba
July 1945 - August 1945

A SLEEPY ATMOSPHERE PREVAILED at No. 10 SFTS in Souris. No aircraft were flying, and the Harvards on the ground were kept in the hangars, untouched. No students were left in the school, and the few administrative staff people were primarily there to see to the needs of the different tradesmen such as myself. In the wireless shop I found a WO2 DeBare, who knew my old friend WO2 Unit quite well. They had been on the same course back in pre-war days. Amenities over, DeBare told me that the main chore in Souris would be the division of the various pieces of equipment into three categories: serviceable and ready for immediate use; unserviceable but able to be overhauled or repaired; and unserviceable beyond repair, or scrap. Once everything had been categorized, someone from Command would verify our findings, and the whole lot would be shipped out to supply depots, repair depots, and scrap heaps as appropriate. As it later turned out, in our case no one from Command had to come in. I had been designated AID (Aircraft or Air Force Inspection Directorate) at Claresholm because I wasn't in charge of an inventory. AIDs were given the authority to designate items of stores as serviceable or otherwise prior to the shipment of such equipment to a depot. As it was DeBare who held the inventory at Souris, Command replied to our signal that the equipment was ready to ship with the instruction for me to certify it and ship it to the relevant depots.

The job was uneventful; slowly but surely all gear was assembled and catalogued. Much of it was in mint condition, which made our job easy. Everything else had to be tested, a time-consuming, tedious operation. We had a few aircraftmen doing some of the dirty work for us, but most of the technical work had to be done by ourselves, as our signatures would be on the equipment tags. The other tradesmen on the station were doing jobs similar to mine. We tried to break up the monotony of the evenings by going to town for whatever excitement might be available, but that was very little.

No. 10 Service Flying Training School 107

The war in the Pacific was proceeding rapidly toward its conclusion, and there was no indication that anyone at Souris would be required for the Pacific force. When the equipment categorization had been completed, DeBare and I received a signal from Command that we were to check out the station sound truck and fully acquaint ourselves with its operation. To the best of my knowledge, sound trucks were only allotted to SFTS's; we never had one at No. 3 B&G School nor at No. 3 WS. The sound truck, a van or panel truck, was used mainly to play music for marching. There were no tape recorders in those days to play the music for us, just records or films with soundtracks. Records were not only delicate, but the motion of the truck would cause the needle to bounce—an impossible situation for marching, as the beat changes dramatically with every bump in the road! Film was the answer for the sound truck, yet this presented another problem. Movie projectors were operated on 110 volts AC, which was normally unobtainable in a truck. The solution was a rotary converter—a battery-driven motor which drove a generator, which developed the AC power required to operate the projector. As we needed sound only, without any picture, the load on the rotary converter was reduced, but a rather large amplifier was necessary to drive the speakers mounted on the top of the truck. All this required an impressive collection of batteries. These were placed in a wooden box, lead-lined so that an acid spill would not go through the box and eventually through the floor boards of the vehicle. From what I can recollect, either four or six large 240-ampere hour batteries were used in parallel, so we had at least 960 and possibly 1440 ampere hours of battery available. The projector and amplifier drew about 40 amperes at maximum load, so they could only be operated for about 24 to 36 hours . . . if the batteries were in 100 percent top condition and fully charged! And, as battery efficiency is affected by temperature, the life of the batteries also depended upon weather conditions, which were often far from perfect.

We had a number of films of British bands, Scottish bands, Irish bands, Canadian bands, and one of the RCAF Central Band. It was not easy to get the system to work, as it had been let slide over the years and was in need of a small overhaul and some refurbishing. DeBare and I knew little about movie projectors, but soon learned. When the system was finally working to our complete satisfaction, we advised No. 2 Training Command HQ.

108   The War Years

To get away from the same faces every evening, DeBare and I occasionally had dinner out. There was a respectable hotel in town of which the manager was justly proud, for he had an excellent dining room. Unfortunately, he had a staff shortage, but he decided that a simple three or four station speaker-type intercom system would solve some of the problems the shortage entailed. I always wore my wireless sparks, and these must have been what prompted him to speak to us about his problem. I had made a few similar intercom systems for No. 3 B&GS and had a rough idea of what it would cost. Yet when I suggested that he might not want to spend that much money, he brushed my objection aside with the remark that money was of little importance. It *was* important to give his clients good service despite the reduced help. So, had we any idea where such a system might be obtained?

It would be no real problem for us to manufacture one from scratch, but we were naturally not prepared to lay out any cash for the cost of a part-finding trip to Winnipeg, and so on. We quickly struck a bargain. The restaurant manager agreed to finance the trip and pay for all necessary parts, plus a certain sum extra for our trouble, if we would manufacture the device. After I made a quick trip to Winnipeg, it took just a few days for DeBare and I to assemble the system and install it in the hotel. The manager was so delighted, he threw in dinners once a week for the next three weeks as a bonus. It was a good deal for us all.

Shortly after this little episode, a signal came from Command for me to wind up my specific AID duties and be prepared to drive the sound truck to No. 2 TCHQ Winnipeg at an hour's notice. It took me little time to clean up the odds and ends of my AID duties, as there was next to nothing left to do, and a day or so later I was advised that I would be "on hold" for at least a week. The full implication of this didn't hit me until a few days later, when I was called in by the Adjutant to be told that I was subject to release. Ottawa, in its wisdom, had decided that the Air Force didn't need me and was prepared to release me to civilian life. I was tempted to take the release, but figured that as soon as I took it, the Army would lay claim to me! I told the Adjutant my thoughts, and she said she would phone Ottawa herself, rather than use signals, to find out where I stood. Sure enough, she called me back in the next day to tell me there had been a mix-up. The previous order regarding my release was cancelled. I had already telephoned Es to tell her of the situation. Her mother and dad were visiting in St. Catharines at the time, and naturally she talked it over with them. I had reminded her of the offer from the Winnipeg radio station, something I might be able to take up if I left the service. As it turned out, her father and I agreed that as I had a number of pensionable years in and was relatively happy in the service, it was probably best if I stuck it out. I gave that information to the Adjutant the next day, and she pulled out some papers for me to sign. A few strokes of the pen and it was all over—I was in the Air Force to stay! WO2 DeBare and I split a small bottle of apricot brandy that night (it was the only drink I enjoyed) to celebrate my continuance in the RCAF.

The next morning I was again called in by the Adjutant, and this time I was very wary! What changes had come from Ottawa? But it wasn't Ottawa, it was Command, demanding that I expedite my departure from Souris and report to a specific officer at a specific location at No. 2 TCHQ immediately. I left Souris post-haste in the lumbering panel truck. The specified officer met me when I arrived in Winnipeg, inquired into the serviceability of the vehicle's equipment, appeared satisfied, and led me to the Senior NCOs quarters, where I was to be billeted until further notice. Under no circumstances was I to leave the area without posting a telephone number where I could be reached, and so forth.

Rumours were circulating that V-J Day was in the wind, and indeed it was. On the 10th of August 1945, I received a call telling me to get the sound truck ready to drive around the camp. I would play band music, and one of the officers, speaking for the AOC (oh, what a wonderful thing a tape recorder would have been!), would tell all and sundry of victory over Japan, the complete cessation of hostilities, and a 48-hour pass for all personnel who were not on essential duties. (Of course, I was one of those on essential duties!)

The next day was a repetition of the first, and I was held in Winnipeg for about a week. The vehicle had to be plugged in every night so the batteries would maintain full charge, or it would have meant my head. As it was, I had a dud battery, but fortunately managed to obtain a replacement from the Motor Transport flight sergeant in one of his better moments. I thought I could at last relax when things wound down at Winnipeg, but it was not so. I was shipped off to Shilo, to let the Army have a whack at using the truck, and then off to Rivers. By then I had had enough of those films, every one of them was indelibly etched on my memory. Finally I was sent back to Souris to get my kit together and await instructions for posting or transfer to another unit. Souris was closing down, and the RCAF was beginning to wind down operations for the post-war years.

Epilogue

WELL, WORLD WAR TWO WAS OVER. I had committed myself to remaining in the RCAF, but was temporarily in limbo. Where was I to go from here? What would my new situation in the RCAF do to or for me and my wife? These questions really concerned me. I knew all about the pre-war services, but post-war was a completely new state of affairs. We assumed there would be a much larger regular military force, and I knew I wanted to be a part of it. The big question was whether I would be able to live in the new environment that would be created.

All sorts of stories had floated about regarding barracks life in the RCAF, yet I had never met any airman who had been a married man living in barracks prior to the war. Only time would tell whether Es and I would enjoy it, but we had endured the war years and come out none the worse for wear, despite living under somewhat adverse conditions. I believed we should be able to survive at least one tour (which we had been advised would last five years) under the new regime.

There was no real indication of where or in what direction the RCAF was going, at least, not to we airmen. We had a great many aircraft and stores of equipment, but not as many men as I had supposed, for most of the wartime enlistees were anxious to resume their civilian jobs, or, at any rate, get out of the service. On the other hand, I considered that a job in the hand was worth much more than one in the bush. The civilian employers who had indicated an interest in hiring me were under no obligation to do so. Most had personnel who had filled the jobs of those chaps who had gone into the military, and why should they fire or release those people to rehire previous employees who had gone to war? Almost all industries had advanced significantly, and retraining the old staff would be expensive and not always desirable. Oh yes, there was something of a moral obligation toward their former employees, but we all know what happens to morality when one must choose between that and the pocketbook!

The electronics industry in Canada was barely underway, and I knew there was a definite future in that field, but I also knew that without a personal contact, the chance of being able to demonstrate your particular expertise was slim. The RCAF, the Army, and the Navy would be using the latest developments in this new technology, and continue to use them. Remaining with them would be the best way to stay current, and be current when retirement finally came my way. I was firm in my decision to stay in, at least for an initial five-year trial.

Book Two of *The RCAF As Seen From the Ground—The Postwar Years*—describes our travels in the so-called interim force. The RCAF was shaking itself into a state of readiness to take on the role it was to play in the peacetime years. Those interim years, from the winter of 1945 to 1952, were crucial for many of us who stayed in the RCAF. We discovered that retraining was necessary not only for those who returned to civilian life, but also for those of us who were to man the new RCAF.

In the years to come I was to travel all across Canada, from as far north as Whitehorse in the Yukon Territory to Clinton in southwestern Ontario, and a number of points in between. By 1952 the RCAF had established itself as a credible organization. Personnel had been trained in all phases of modern technology and our peacetime role had been firmly established.

It appeared to me that I had a future in the RCAF and I only hoped that Es would see it that way as well. She did, and we were to fully enjoy our years in the interim force. But that's another story!

Glossary

Glossary

A/C Air Commodore; see **rank structure**
AC2 or **AC1** Aircraftman Second or First Class; see **rank structure**
AEM aero-engine mechanic, or fitter
AFAO Air Force administrative orders, standard at all stations.
AFHQ Air Force Headquarters (Ottawa)
AFM airframe mechanic, or rigger
AFP Air Force police; also called service police
AGLT automatic gun-laying turret
AID Air Force Inspection Directorate
AM amplitude modulation
AMES 11 Air Ministry Experimental Station, Mark 11
AMCHQ Air Materiel Command Headquarters
ANS air navigators school
AOC Air Oficer Commanding; the officer in charge of a Command
AOS air observers school
AR4 battery-operated special communications receiver
armourer armament tradesman
ATC Air Transport Command
ATCHQ Air Training Command Headquarters
attention area area adjacent to a station's flag pole through which all personnel were expected to pass at attention; that is, there was to be no talking, smoking, chewing gum, etc, in that area
AT1/AR2 and **AR6/AT7** RCAF communications equipment (1940)
ATR5/ATR8 RCAF transmitter/receiver
AT3 RCAF ground transmitter (1940)
AvGas high-octane aviation gasoline
B&GS bombing and gunnery school
Barbour's twine waxed cord used for lacing wires together
BCATP British Commonwealth Air Training Plan
BCI broadcast interference
brass military jargon for important or high-ranking people
BSM Battery Sergeant Major (artillery)
canteen, wet/dry the wet canteen sold beer, liquor, and snacks; the dry canteen sold other commodities, such as soft drinks, ice cream, stationery, etc.

115

CAPs Canadian Air Publications
CAP90 drill manual
CASF Canadian Active Service Force, formed in September 1939 to supplement the Canadian Permanent Armed Forces
CD Canadian Forces Decoration, awarded for twelve years service; a bar (or clasp) was additionally awarded for every additional six years
CE construction engineering; see **W&B**
Central Warehouse establishment at most RCAF stations that purchased commodities to be sold in the messes and canteens. A non-public venture controlled by the SAO, it was normally a well organized unit.
CH chain home; radar with fixed antennae that searched for high-flying aircraft
CHL chain home (low); radar with fixed antennae that searched for low-flying aircraft
chopper slang for helicopter
Chieffie (from RAF) fond or familiar nickname for flight sergeant
chute slang for parachute
civvies civilian clothing or, in some cases, civilian personnel
CI Chief Instructor
CO Commanding Officer, usually the senior officer of a station
come-along device used by linesmen and electricians to tighten wire; a block and tackle plus a pair of cable clamps
Coventry or **to place a man in Coventry** English expression; to give a man the silent treatment.
Cpl Corporal
crash truck unit vehicles used at the scene of a crash: ambulance, fire truck, etc.
CTSO Chief Technical Services Officer
CTelO Command Telecommunications Officer
CT cease training; to be taken off course, either by request or by order
CW continuous wave (used in Morse)
DAPS Directorate of Air Personnel Services
D8 or **Don8** field telephone wire; used for its great strength; seven strands of steel and one of copper were twisted together, coated with rubber, and covered with linen.
Discip disciplinarian; drill sergeant
DOC Department of Communications
DOT Department of Transport
dope shop workshop in which fabric used in aircraft was repaired or coated with protective dope
DROs Daily Routine Orders
drone small, remote-controlled aircraft used as a target
drogue large cloth or nylon sleeve towed behind an aircraft as target

drogue operator non-tradesman who repaired, marked, packed, and collected the drogue, and who operated the towing equipment in the aircraft
drogue aircraft aircraft that towed a drogue
duckwalk temporary sidewalk made in sections for easy movement
dural or **duralumin** aluminium alloy remarkable for its strength and hardness, used for aircraft, etc.
EM Efficiency Medal
EOs Engineering Orders, a standard text describing specific gear
EMQs Emergency Married Quarters, those that are below the standards set in the AFAO
erk slang for very junior airman
E26 repayment voucher, used to reimburse the Crown for lost items
E42 purchase order; document used to obtain items from stores
E52 conversion voucher, used to reduce a number of small items into one major item
featherbedding taking the easy way out
F/F Air Force fire department personnel
fire piquet group of personnel responsible for checking establishment for fire hazards
F/S Flight Sergeant
GD general duties; airmen used for useful duties in any capacity
glycol coolant used in liquid-cooled aircraft engines
GOBC Ground Observer Corps
gong slang for medal
gosport flexible tube used for intercommunication between crew in aircraft
hangar boots felt boots worn in hangars where fabric-covered aircraft were kept
I Card identity card
IFF identification, friend or foe; electronic device in military aircraft which would identify it as Allied to radar
ITS initial training school
Juicer slang for Englishman
KP kitchen police, personnel on kitchen duty; American term
L14 log of all work done on an aircraft
LAC Leading Aircraftman
LPO local purchase order; authority to purchase equipment and charge it to the Crown
MCW modulated continuous wave
MPO military post office
nacelle engine cover
NWAC North West Air Command (Edmonton)
Oi/c officer in charge
OC Officer Commanding
OEM original equipment manufacturer

PAAF Permanent Active Air Force
PAdO personnel administrative officer
PAO pay accounts officer
PF Permanent Force
PIO public information officer
PEng professional engineer
plotting board, horizontal/vertical horizontal board was a map with miniature aircraft, ships, etc., showing assumed locations; vertical board was a map of clear plastic which could be marked with grease pencil to show the tracks of friendly and hostile aircraft
Plug 58 plug at the end of headset or helmet intercom cord
PRO public relations officer
queen bee slang for the senior WD officer at an establishment
RAF Royal Air Force
RAAF Royal Australian Air Force
RCAF Royal Canadian Air Force
RNZAF Royal New Zealand Air Force
rank structure Aircraftman, 2nd Class; Aircraftman 1st Class; Leading Aircraftman; Corporal; Sergeant; Flight Sergeant; Warrant Officer 2nd Class; Warrant Officer 1st Class; Provisional Pilot Officer; Pilot Officer; Flying Officer; Flight Lieutenant; Squadron Leader; Wing Commander; Group Captain; Air Commodore; Air Vice Marshal; Air Marshal; Air Chief Marshal
RD repair depot
SAC School of Army Co-operation
SAC Strategic Air Command
sand box type of horizontal plotting board
scale of issue number of personnel, buildings, equipment, size of buildings, etc., established for a specific unit
SCR signal corps radio; American term
scrambled eggs slang for the gold braid on officers' field service hats
SFTS service flying training school
Sgt Sergeant
Signals Section shop or division that maintained wireless equipment
Socket 29 companion to the plug 58; mounted in the aircraft
SSOs station standing orders
SWO station warrant officer; the station disciplinarian
TD temporary duty
TelMSupt telecommunications maintenance superintendent
TR9D RAF communications equipment
TTY teletype
VE-Day Victory in Europe; May 8, 1945
VJ-Day Victory in Japan; August 15, 1945
Vocab vocabulary, the RCAF stores catalogue
WAG wireless operator air gunner
WD RCAF Women's Division; a member of same

WEM wireless electrical mechanic, a wartime trade
WM wireless mechanic, a wartime trade
W/Op wireless operator
WOEM wireless operator, electrical mechanic, early wartime trade
Works & Bricks slang for Works & Buildings
W&B Works and Buildings, later Construction Engineering; department that looks after the maintenance of the buildings and lands of the establishment
WS wireless school

RAYMOND H. FOGLER LIBRARY

DATE DUE

BOOKS ARE SUBJECT TO
RECALL AFTER TWO WEEKS